SWEDISH DEATH CLEANING MADE SIMPLE FOR AMERICANS

Learn How to Declutter Your Home, Organize Your Life, and Create a Meaningful Legacy with the Scandinavian Art of Minimalism

Elin Lindström

© Copyright 2024 - All rights reserved.

The content contained within this book may not be reproduced, duplicated, or transmitted without direct written permission from the author or the publisher.

Under no circumstances will any blame or legal responsibility be held against the publisher, or author, for any damages, reparation, or monetary loss due to the information contained within this book. Either directly or indirectly.

Legal Notice:

This book is copyright protected. This book is only for personal use. You cannot amend, distribute, sell, use, quote, or paraphrase any part, or the content within this book, without the consent of the author or publisher.

Disclaimer Notice:

By reading this document, the reader agrees that under no circumstances is the author responsible for any losses, direct or indirect, which are incurred as a result of the use of the information contained within this document, including, but not limited to, — errors, omissions, or inaccuracies.

Table Of

CONTENTS

PREFACE

In our modern world, we are often overwhelmed by the sheer volume of things we accumulate over time. Our homes, once a haven of peace and tranquility, can become cluttered with items that hold sentimental value but also contribute to a sense of chaos and disorganization. This clutter doesn't just occupy our physical space; it also invades our emotional and mental landscapes, creating stress and preventing us from living our lives to the fullest.

As we age, the issue of clutter becomes more than just an inconvenience. It turns into a burden that we inadvertently pass on to our loved ones. This realization led me to the concept of Swedish Death Cleaning, a practice that, despite its somewhat morose name, is all about celebrating life and making it easier for those we leave behind.

Swedish Death Cleaning, or "döstädning," combines the Swedish words for death and cleaning. It's a process that involves decluttering your life, not just in anticipation of death, but as a way to enhance your life right now. It's about making conscious decisions about what to keep, what to let go of, and how to organize your belongings in a way that reflects the life you want to live.

This book, "Swedish Death Cleaning Made Simple for Americans," is a guide to help you navigate this process. It's not just about getting rid of stuff. It's about understanding why we hold onto things, how to let go, and how to live a more intentional, clutter-free life. It's about creating a legacy that your loved ones can cherish, rather than a burden they must bear.

In the following chapters, we'll explore the principles of Swedish Death Cleaning and how they can be adapted to the American lifestyle. We'll delve into the psychology of letting go, the practicalities of decluttering, and the art of creating a meaningful legacy. We'll also discuss the importance of involving family in the process, maintaining a clutter-free life, and planning for your legacy.

Whether you're in your forties or your seventies, single or married, a parent or grandparent, this book is for you. It's for anyone who wants to simplify their life, create a peaceful living environment, and leave a positive legacy for their loved ones.

This journey may not be easy. Letting go of belongings, especially those with sentimental value, can be emotionally challenging. But I assure you, the rewards are worth it. As you declutter your home, you'll also declutter your mind and soul. You'll create space for personal growth, peace, and well-being. You'll enhance your life and the lives of those you love.

So, let's embark on this journey together. Let's explore the art of Swedish Death Cleaning and discover how it can transform your life and legacy. Let's make the process of decluttering simple, manageable, and meaningful. Let's create a home and a life that reflects who we are and what we value most.

Welcome to "Swedish Death Cleaning Made Simple for Americans." Let's begin.

Elin Lindström

Introduction

EMBRACING THE JOURNEY OF SWEDISH DEATH CLEANING

1. What is Swedish Death Cleaning?

The concept of Swedish Death Cleaning may initially seem morose, but it's far from it. In fact, it's a life-affirming practice that emphasizes the importance of living intentionally and leaving a positive legacy. As we embark on this journey together, let's first understand what Swedish Death Cleaning is and how it can transform our lives.

Swedish Death Cleaning, or "döstädning," is a Scandinavian practice that combines the Swedish words for death ("dö") and cleaning ("städning"). Despite its somewhat ominous name, it's not solely about preparing for death. Instead, it's a method of decluttering that encourages us to simplify our lives, make our homes more manageable, and ease the burden on our loved ones when we are no longer around.

The term was popularized by Margareta Magnusson, a Swedish artist who wrote a book about the practice. Magnusson suggests that people should start death cleaning as they reach their fifties, but the principles are applicable at any age. It's about taking control of your belongings instead of letting them control you.

Swedish Death Cleaning is not just about tidying up; it's a holistic approach to living. It involves going through your belongings, one by one, and deciding what to keep, what to give away, and what to discard. It's about making conscious decisions about what truly matters to you and what you want to leave behind.

This process can be deeply emotional. It often involves parting with items that hold sentimental value or that are tied to specific memories. However, it also provides an opportunity for reflection and reminiscence. It allows you to revisit your past, relive fond memories, and pass on your stories and experiences to the next generation.

Swedish Death Cleaning is not a one-time event; it's a lifelong process. It's about constantly reassessing your belongings and your relationship with them. It's about recognizing that our needs and priorities change over time, and so should our possessions. It's about understanding that less can indeed be more, and that a clutter-free home can lead to a clutter-free mind.

Moreover, Swedish Death Cleaning is not just about physical clutter. It also involves decluttering our digital lives, sorting out our paperwork, and even addressing our unfinished business. It's about creating a sense of order and peace, not just in our homes, but in all aspects of our lives.

In essence, Swedish Death Cleaning is about living with intentionality. It's about curating a life that reflects our values, our passions, and our legacy. It's about creating a home that feels like a sanctuary, not a storage unit. It's about making our remaining years more enjoyable and less burdened by stuff.

As we delve deeper into the concept and practice of Swedish Death Cleaning, remember that it's not a race or a competition. It's a personal journey that takes time, patience, and compassion. It's about progress, not perfection. It's about making small, consistent changes that add up to big transformations.

Let's approach it with an open mind and an open heart. Let's embrace the opportunity to reflect, to let go, and to choose what we want our lives and our legacy to be. Let's discover the joy and freedom that comes from living less cluttered, more intentional lives.

2. Why Decluttering is a Gift to Yourself and Others

Decluttering is often seen as a practical task, a way to create more space in our homes or to make our lives more organized. But the truth is, decluttering is so much more than that. It's a gift to ourselves and to others, a process that can bring profound benefits to our emotional well-being, our relationships, and our sense of self.

When we declutter, we are not just getting rid of unnecessary items. We are making space for what truly matters. We are clearing away the physical and emotional clutter that can weigh us down and prevent us from living fully. We are creating a home that reflects our true selves, our values, and our aspirations. In this way, decluttering is a form of self-care, a way to nurture ourselves and create a peaceful, supportive environment.

Decluttering can also be a powerful tool for personal growth. As we sort through our belongings, we are forced to confront our past, our memories, and our attachments. We have to make decisions about what to keep and what to let go of, decisions that require us to reflect on our lives and our priorities. This process can be challenging, but it can also be deeply rewarding. It can help us gain clarity about who we are, what we value, and what we want our lives to look like.

But the benefits of decluttering extend beyond our own well-being. When we declutter, we are also giving a gift to others. By reducing our possessions, we are easing the burden on our loved ones who would otherwise have to sort through our belongings after we're gone. We are leaving behind a clean, organized home that reflects our love and respect for them.

Moreover, decluttering can also benefit our community and our planet. When we declutter responsibly, donating or recycling items instead of throwing them away, we are contributing to a more sustainable, equitable world. We are giving our belongings a second life, reducing waste, and supporting those in need.

In the context of Swedish Death Cleaning, decluttering becomes an even more meaningful process. It's not just about creating a tidy home or reducing our environmental footprint. It's about preparing for the end of life, making peace with our mortality, and creating a meaningful legacy.

When we engage in Swedish Death Cleaning, we are not just sorting through our possessions. We are reflecting on our lives, our memories, and our relationships. We are sharing our stories, passing on our wisdom, and expressing our love for our loved ones. We are making decisions about our legacy, deciding what we want to leave behind and how we want to be remembered.

In this way, Swedish Death Cleaning is a deeply emotional, deeply personal process. It's a process that requires courage, honesty, and compassion. But it's also a process that can bring immense rewards. It can bring us a sense of peace, clarity, and fulfillment. It can strengthen our connections with our loved ones. And it can help us create a legacy that reflects our true selves, our values, and our love for others.

So, why declutter? Why engage in Swedish Death Cleaning? Because it's a gift. A gift to ourselves, a gift to our loved ones, and a gift to our world. It's a gift of space, clarity, and peace. It's a gift of love, connection, and legacy. And ultimately, it's a gift of a simpler, more intentional, more fulfilling life.

As we embark on this journey of Swedish Death Cleaning, we'll explore the practical steps of decluttering, the emotional challenges and rewards, and the profound impact it can have on our lives and our legacy. We'll learn how to declutter in a way that honors our past, reflects our present, and prepares for our future. And we'll discover how this simple, compassionate practice can transform our homes, our relationships, and our lives. So, let's continue this journey together, embracing the gift of decluttering and the promise of a meaningful, clutter-free legacy.

3. Preparing for Your Death Cleaning Journey

It's important to approach the process with the right mindset and a well-thought-out plan. This journey is not just about decluttering; it's about reflecting on our lives, our values, and our legacy. It's about making conscious decisions about what we want to keep, what we want to let go of, and what we want to leave behind.

The first step in preparing for your Swedish Death Cleaning journey is to understand your motivations. Why do you want to declutter? Is it to create a more peaceful and manageable living environment? Is it to ease the burden on your loved ones? Is it to live a more intentional and mindful life? Understanding your motivations will help you stay focused and committed throughout the process.

Next, it's important to set realistic expectations. Swedish Death Cleaning is not a quick fix; it's a gradual process that takes time, patience, and emotional energy. Don't expect to declutter your entire home in a weekend. Instead, plan to tackle one area at a time, starting with the easiest and gradually moving on to the more challenging areas. Remember, the goal is not just to declutter, but to reflect, reminisce, and make conscious decisions about your belongings.

As you prepare for your journey, consider involving your family and loved ones in the process. Swedish Death Cleaning is not just about your belongings; it's about your life and your legacy. Involving your loved ones can strengthen your relationships, create shared memories, and ensure a shared understanding of your wishes. It can also make the process more enjoyable and less overwhelming.

Another crucial aspect of preparation is dealing with potential obstacles. One common obstacle is emotional attachment to belongings, as we've discussed earlier. Another obstacle might be the sheer volume of items to go through. Yet another might be the physical effort required, especially if you're older or have health issues. Identifying these obstacles upfront can help you come up with strategies to overcome them.

One effective strategy is to break the process down into manageable tasks. Instead of thinking about decluttering your entire home, focus on one room, one closet, or even one drawer at a time. Celebrate your progress along the way, no matter how small.

Another strategy is to create a system for sorting your belongings. One popular method is the four-box method, where you have a box for items to keep, items to donate or sell, items to throw away, and items to decide on later. This can make the process more organized and less overwhelming.

Finally, as you prepare for your Swedish Death Cleaning journey, remember to take care of yourself. This process can be emotionally and physically draining. Make sure to take breaks, eat well, get plenty of rest, and do things you enjoy. Remember, this journey is not just about decluttering; it's about enhancing your well-being and quality of life.

Preparing for your Swedish Death Cleaning journey involves understanding your motivations, setting realistic expectations, involving your loved ones, dealing with potential obstacles, breaking the process down into manageable tasks, creating a sorting system, and taking care of yourself. With these preparations in place, you'll be well-equipped to embark on this transformative journey.

Swedish Death Cleaning is not about death; it's about life. It's about living intentionally, creating a peaceful living environment, and leaving a positive legacy. It's about choosing what truly matters to you and letting go of the rest. So, as you prepare for this journey, embrace the opportunity to reflect, to let go, and to choose the life and legacy you want. Let's embark on this journey together.

Chapter 1

THE PSYCHOLOGY OF LETTING GO

1. Emotional Attachments and Sentimental Clutter

One of the first and most significant hurdles we encounter is dealing with emotional attachments and sentimental clutter. These items, imbued with memories and emotions, often hold a special place in our hearts, making the process of letting go challenging. However, understanding the psychology behind these attachments can provide us with the tools needed to navigate this process successfully.

Our belongings are more than just physical objects. They are vessels of memories, symbols of relationships, and markers of our personal history. A piece of jewelry might remind us of a cherished family member, a stack of old letters might take us back to our younger days, and a collection of photos might chronicle our life's milestones. These items, rich in sentimental value, often become an integral part of our identity, making the thought of parting with them feel like losing a piece of ourselves.

This emotional attachment to our belongings is deeply ingrained in our psychology. According to attachment theory, we are biologically programmed to form attachments as a means of survival. While this theory primarily refers to our relationships with people, it can also apply to our relationships with objects. Our belongings provide us with a sense of security, continuity, and identity, especially in times of change or uncertainty.

However, when our sentimental items start to accumulate and create clutter, they can also contribute to stress and overwhelm. What was once a source of comfort can become a source of anxiety. Our homes, meant to be our sanctuaries, can start to feel crowded and chaotic. Our belongings, meant to enrich our lives, can start to burden them.

The key to dealing with emotional attachments and sentimental clutter is to strike a balance. It's about learning to honor our memories and emotions without letting them take over our physical space and mental peace. It's about distinguishing between the items that truly add value to our lives and the items that merely add to our clutter.

One effective strategy is to practice mindful decluttering. Instead of impulsively discarding items, take the time to hold each item, reflect on its significance, and make a conscious decision about its fate. This process, though time-consuming, can make the act of letting go more meaningful and less distressing.

Another strategy is to keep a representative sample of sentimental items. For instance, instead of keeping all your children's artwork, select a few pieces that capture their creativity and growth. Instead of holding onto every gift from a loved one, choose a few that hold the most meaning. This approach allows you to honor your memories without overwhelming your space.

Letting go of an item does not mean letting go of the memory associated with it. Memories reside within us, not within our belongings. By letting go of the physical item, we are not erasing the memory; we are merely making space for new memories and experiences.

It's important to be patient and compassionate with yourself. Letting go of emotional attachments is not easy. It's a process that requires time, patience, and emotional resilience. It's perfectly okay to feel a sense of loss or grief as you part with your sentimental items. Allow yourself to feel these emotions, but also remind yourself of the peace and freedom that comes with decluttering.

Dealing with emotional attachments and sentimental clutter is a crucial part of the Swedish Death Cleaning process. It's a journey of self-discovery, reflection, and letting go. It's about honoring our past, making peace with our present, and making room for our future. It's about choosing to live a life not weighed down by clutter, but enriched by meaningful memories and experiences.

2. Facing the Fear of Decluttering

As we delve deeper into the psychology of letting go, it's essential to address a common obstacle that many of us face: the fear of decluttering. This fear can take many forms, from the fear of making wrong decisions and regretting them later, to the fear of losing memories, to the fear of confronting our emotions. Understanding and addressing these fears is a crucial step in our Swedish Death Cleaning journey.

The fear of decluttering often stems from a sense of uncertainty. When we declutter, we're forced to make decisions about our belongings. We have to decide what to keep, what to give away, and what to discard. These decisions can be challenging, especially when we're dealing with sentimental items. We might fear making the wrong decision, parting with something we might need or want in the future, or regretting our choices later.

This fear of making wrong decisions can be paralyzing. It can prevent us from starting the decluttering process or cause us to procrastinate. It can make us second-guess ourselves and create a sense of anxiety and overwhelm.

One way to overcome this fear is to remind ourselves that decluttering is not a one-time event, but a continuous process. We're not expected to make perfect decisions all the time. It's okay to make mistakes, to change our minds, or to revisit our decisions. What's important is that we're making progress, learning from our experiences, and moving towards a less cluttered and more intentional life.

Another common fear is the fear of losing memories. We often associate our belongings with specific memories, experiences, or people. Parting with these items can feel like parting with our memories. We might fear that once the item is gone, the memory will be gone too.

However, it's important to remember that memories reside within us, not within our belongings. We can let go of the physical item without losing the memory. In fact, the act of decluttering can often enhance our memories, as we're forced to revisit and reflect on them. We can also find creative ways to preserve our memories, such as taking photos of our items, writing about them, or sharing our stories with our loved ones.

A third type of fear is the fear of confronting our emotions. Decluttering is not just a physical process; it's also an emotional one. It requires us to face our past, confront our feelings, and deal with any unresolved issues. This emotional aspect of decluttering can be challenging and even painful. We might fear what we'll uncover, how we'll react, or how we'll cope.

To face this fear, it's important to approach decluttering with a sense of compassion and self-care. Allow yourself to feel your emotions, but also remind yourself that it's okay to let go. Take breaks when needed, seek support from loved ones, and celebrate your progress along the way. Remember, decluttering is not about creating a perfect home or life; it's about creating a home and life that feels good to you.

Facing the fear of decluttering is a crucial step in our Swedish Death Cleaning journey. It's about acknowledging our fears, understanding their roots, and finding ways to overcome them. It's about embracing the uncertainty, the emotions, and the challenges that come with decluttering. It's about choosing to face our fears, to let go of our clutter, and to create a life that reflects our values, our passions, and our legacy. It's about choosing courage over fear, progress over perfection, and intentionality over clutter.

3. Creating a Positive Mindset for Decluttering

One of the most powerful tools at our disposal is our mindset. Our mindset shapes how we perceive and respond to the world around us. It influences our thoughts, our feelings, and our actions. Therefore, creating a positive mindset for decluttering is a crucial part of our Swedish Death Cleaning journey.

A positive mindset is not about ignoring or denying the challenges of decluttering. It's not about pretending that letting go is easy or that we don't have any emotional attachments to our belongings. Instead, a positive mindset is about acknowledging these challenges and choosing to focus on the benefits and possibilities that decluttering brings.

Creating a positive mindset for decluttering starts with reframing our perspective. Instead of viewing decluttering as a daunting task, we can choose to see it as an opportunity. It's an opportunity to reassess our belongings, to reflect on our lives, and to make conscious decisions about what we want to keep, what we want to let go of, and what we want to leave behind.

This reframing also involves focusing on the benefits of decluttering. Decluttering can create a more peaceful and manageable living environment. It can reduce stress, increase productivity, and enhance our well-being. It can free us from the burden of excess and allow us to live more intentionally and mindfully.

Another aspect of creating a positive mindset is embracing the process. Decluttering is not just about the end result; it's about the journey. It's about the insights we gain, the memories we revisit, and the emotions we process along the way. By embracing the process, we can find joy and fulfillment in each step, no matter how small.

Creating a positive mindset also involves practicing self-compassion. Decluttering can be an emotional and challenging process. It's normal to feel overwhelmed, to make mistakes, or to struggle with letting go. Instead of criticizing ourselves for these struggles, we can choose to be kind and patient with ourselves. We can acknowledge our feelings, validate our experiences, and remind ourselves that we're doing the best we can.

Finally, creating a positive mindset involves cultivating a sense of gratitude. Gratitude can shift our focus from what we're losing to what we're gaining. It can help us appreciate the items we choose to keep, the memories we cherish, and the space we create. It can also help us appreciate our progress, our efforts, and our courage in embarking on this journey.

Creating a positive mindset for decluttering is a crucial part of our Swedish Death Cleaning journey. It's about reframing our perspective, focusing on the benefits, embracing the process, practicing self-compassion, and cultivating gratitude. With this positive mindset, we can navigate the challenges of decluttering, honor our emotional attachments, and create a life and home that reflect our values, our passions, and our legacy.

Our mindset is not fixed; it's something we can choose and shape. By choosing a positive mindset, we're choosing to see the possibilities, to embrace the journey, and to create a positive, lasting change in our lives. So, as we continue on this journey, let's choose to focus on the positive, to embrace the process, and to celebrate our progress. Let's choose to create a mindset that supports and empowers us in our Swedish Death Cleaning journey.

4. The Role of Family Heirlooms and Legacy Items

In the landscape of our belongings, certain items stand out with a distinct aura of their own. These are our family heirlooms and legacy items, objects that carry the weight of generations, narrate family histories, and symbolize our personal legacies. As we navigate the process of Swedish Death Cleaning, understanding the role and significance of these items becomes crucial.

Family heirlooms and legacy items are often deeply intertwined with our sense of identity and belonging. They connect us to our roots, our heritage, and our ancestors. They tell stories of love, resilience, and accomplishment. They are physical embodiments of our family's history and our place within that narrative. A grandmother's locket, a father's favorite book, a piece of furniture passed down through generations - these items are more than just objects; they are links to our past and bridges to our future.

However, these items can also present unique challenges when it comes to decluttering. Their sentimental and historical value can make the decision to keep or let go particularly difficult. We might feel a sense of duty or obligation to preserve these items, even if they no longer serve a practical purpose in our lives or align with our personal style or values.

One of the key aspects of dealing with family heirlooms and legacy items is understanding that while these items carry history and sentiment, they do not hold the exclusive rights to our memories or our family's legacy. The memories and stories exist within us and our shared familial knowledge, independent of the physical objects. Releasing an heirloom does not erase the history it represents.

When considering what to do with these items, it can be helpful to ask yourself a few questions. Does this item bring me joy or does it feel more like a burden? Does it align with the life I am currently living or hope to live? Is there someone else in the family who might value this item more? Honest answers to these questions can guide your decision-making process and help you navigate the emotional complexities tied to these items.

If an heirloom doesn't fit your life but you're hesitant about letting it go, consider other ways to preserve its memory. Photograph the item, write down the stories associated with it, or even create a digital archive of your family heirlooms. This way, you can keep the history and sentiment alive without holding onto the physical item.

When it comes to passing on your own legacy items, be mindful of not creating a burden for your loved ones. Open a dialogue with your family members about these items. Understand their feelings, their preferences, and their lifestyle before passing on an item. The goal of Swedish Death Cleaning is to ease the burden on your loved ones, and that includes thoughtful consideration of what legacy items to pass on.

Family heirlooms and legacy items play a significant role in our decluttering journey. They connect us to our past, contribute to our identity, and carry forward our family's legacy. However, they can also complicate the decluttering process due to their emotional and historical significance. By understanding their role, asking the right questions, preserving memories in alternative ways, and considering our loved ones' perspectives, we can navigate these complexities and make thoughtful decisions about these special items.

The goal of Swedish Death Cleaning is not to erase our past, but to honor it in a way that serves our present and future. It's about choosing what to carry forward and what to let go. It's about curating a life that reflects who we are, who we've been, and who we aspire to be. And that includes making conscious decisions about our family heirlooms and legacy items.

5. Empowering Yourself Through Minimalism

As we delve further into the psychology of letting go, a powerful concept emerges that can guide and empower us on our decluttering journey: minimalism. Minimalism, at its core, is about living with less in order to live more. It's about letting go of excess, distraction, and clutter to make room for what truly matters. It's about choosing quality over quantity, intentionality over mindless accumulation, and presence over possessions.

Embracing minimalism does not mean living in an empty house or renouncing all material possessions. Rather, it's about creating a space and a life that reflect our values, our passions, and our purpose. It's about consciously choosing what to bring into our lives and what to let go of. It's about understanding that our worth is not defined by what we own, but by who we are and how we live.

Minimalism can be a powerful tool in our Swedish Death Cleaning journey. It can help us navigate the emotional challenges of decluttering, make conscious decisions about our belongings, and create a home and life that feel authentic and fulfilling. It can empower us to take control of our environment, our time, and our energy.

When we choose minimalism, we choose to let go of the clutter that's weighing us down. We choose to let go of the items that no longer serve us, the items that are taking up space without adding value to our lives. We choose to let go of the stress, the overwhelm, and the distraction that come with excess.

But more importantly, we choose what to keep. We choose the items that bring us joy, that serve a purpose, that align with our values. We choose the items that tell our story, that reflect our identity, that contribute to our well-being. We choose the items that make our house feel like a home.

By empowering ourselves through minimalism, we're not just decluttering our homes; we're decluttering our lives. We're creating space for growth, for peace, for creativity. We're making room for new experiences, new memories, and new possibilities.

Empowering ourselves through minimalism is a vital part of our Swedish Death Cleaning journey. It's about choosing less in order to live more. It's about letting go of the excess to make room for what truly matters. It's about creating a life that reflects our values, our passions, and our legacy. So, as we continue on this journey, let's choose to empower ourselves through minimalism. Let's choose to live a life that feels authentic, intentional, and fulfilling.

Chapter 2

THE AMERICAN HOME AND SWEDISH DEATH CLEANING

1. Adapting Swedish Practices to the American Lifestyle

We are now faced with the task of adapting these practices to fit the American lifestyle. The Swedish concept of 'döstädning', which combines the words for death ('dö') and cleaning ('städning'), may initially seem foreign or even morbid to an American audience. However, when we delve deeper into the philosophy behind it, we find universal principles that can be seamlessly integrated into our lives, regardless of our cultural background.

Swedish Death Cleaning is about more than just decluttering; it's about mindful living, intentional ownership, and thoughtful legacy planning. It's about creating a home and life that reflect our values, our passions, and our legacy. It's about reducing the burden on our loved ones and ensuring that our belongings tell the story we want to be remembered by. These principles align well with the American values of individuality, responsibility, and forward-thinking.

The first step in adapting Swedish Death Cleaning to the American lifestyle is understanding the differences and similarities between the two cultures. The Swedish lifestyle tends to be more minimalist and eco-conscious, with a strong emphasis on functionality and quality over quantity. The American lifestyle, on the other hand, often leans towards consumerism, with larger homes and a greater accumulation of belongings.

However, there is a growing trend in America towards minimalism, sustainability, and intentional living. More and more Americans are recognizing the benefits of decluttering, not just for their physical space, but also for their mental and emotional well-being. They are seeking ways to reduce stress, increase productivity, and enhance their quality of life. Swedish Death Cleaning, with its focus on mindful decluttering and legacy planning, fits well into this trend.

Adapting Swedish Death Cleaning to the American lifestyle also involves addressing the practical aspects of decluttering. American homes, often larger than their Swedish counterparts, may require more time and effort to declutter. The process may need to be broken down into smaller, more manageable tasks, and spread out over a longer period of time.

Additionally, the American culture of consumerism may present unique challenges. The constant influx of new items, driven by sales, trends, and the desire for the latest gadgets, can make it harder to maintain a decluttered home. This calls for conscious consumption, regular decluttering, and strong decision-making skills.

Adapting Swedish Death Cleaning to the American lifestyle is about integrating the principles of mindful living, intentional ownership, and thoughtful legacy planning into our lives. It's about recognizing the benefits of decluttering, addressing the practical challenges, and making conscious choices that align with our values and lifestyle. It's about creating a home and life that not only reflect who we are, but also who we aspire to be. So, as we continue on this journey, let's embrace the Swedish concept of Death Cleaning and adapt it to fit our unique American lifestyle.

2. Navigating Consumer Culture

The American lifestyle, with its strong consumer culture, can present a unique set of challenges when it comes to Swedish Death Cleaning. We live in a society that often equates success and happiness with material possessions. We're constantly bombarded with advertisements encouraging us to buy more, to own the latest gadgets, to keep up with the latest trends. This culture of consumerism can lead to an accumulation of belongings, making the process of decluttering more daunting.

However, Swedish Death Cleaning offers a powerful antidote to this consumer culture. It encourages us to reassess our relationship with our belongings, to question our consumption habits, and to make more conscious and intentional choices. It invites us to shift our focus from quantity to quality, from mindless accumulation to mindful ownership.

Navigating consumer culture while practicing Swedish Death Cleaning involves several key strategies. First, it's important to become more aware of our consumption habits. This involves noticing our shopping triggers, such as sales, advertisements, or emotional states, and finding healthier ways to respond to them. It also involves questioning our purchases, asking ourselves whether we truly need an item, whether it adds value to our lives, and whether it aligns with our values and goals.

Second, it's crucial to adopt a mindset of enough. In a culture that constantly encourages us to want more, it can be empowering to recognize that we already have enough. This doesn't mean denying ourselves of new purchases, but rather making sure that each purchase is intentional, purposeful, and adds genuine value to our lives.

Third, navigating consumer culture involves developing strong decision-making skills. This includes the ability to say no to unnecessary purchases, to let go of items that no longer serve us, and to make conscious choices about what we bring into our homes and lives. It also includes the ability to deal with the guilt, regret, or fear that can sometimes accompany these decisions.

Finally, navigating consumer culture involves regular decluttering. Given the constant influx of new items, it's important to regularly reassess our belongings and let go of the ones that no longer serve us. This not only helps maintain a clutter-free home, but also reinforces our new consumption habits and decision-making skills.

Navigating consumer culture is a crucial part of our Swedish Death Cleaning journey. It involves becoming more aware of our consumption habits, adopting a mindset of enough, developing strong decision-making skills, and regularly decluttering. By doing so, we can create a home and life that reflect our values, our passions, and our legacy, rather than the latest trends or advertisements.

Swedish Death Cleaning is not about rejecting consumer culture altogether, but rather about navigating it in a more mindful and intentional way. It's about choosing to consume less so that we can live more. It's about choosing to own less so that we can be more. And it's about choosing to declutter not just our homes, but also our minds and our lives.

3. Family Dynamics and Decluttering

Family dynamics play a significant role in the process of Swedish Death Cleaning, particularly in the context of the American home. Our families are not just the recipients of our legacies; they are also our partners in the journey of decluttering. Understanding and navigating these dynamics can greatly facilitate the process and enhance the outcomes of our decluttering efforts.

In many American families, belongings are not just possessions; they are symbols of memories, milestones, and relationships. They are the physical manifestations of shared histories and collective identities. As such, the process of decluttering can elicit a range of emotions and reactions from family members. It can bring up old memories, stir up latent conflicts, or even trigger feelings of loss or grief.

One of the key aspects of managing family dynamics in decluttering is open communication. It's important to discuss your intentions and goals for decluttering with your family members. Explain the concept of Swedish Death Cleaning and how it can benefit not just you, but the entire family. Encourage them to share their thoughts, feelings, and concerns, and be open to their feedback and suggestions.

Involving family members in the process can also be beneficial. They can provide practical help, emotional support, and valuable perspectives. They can help you make decisions about certain items, share in the reminiscing of old memories, or even take on some of the tasks. Involving them not only eases your burden but also gives them a sense of ownership and investment in the process.

However, it's also important to set boundaries. While it's good to involve family members and consider their feelings, the process of Swedish Death Cleaning is ultimately about your belongings and your legacy. It's okay to make decisions that are right for you, even if others may not fully agree or understand. It's okay to let go of items that no longer serve you, even if they hold sentimental value for others.

Managing family dynamics also involves dealing with the distribution of belongings. This can be a sensitive issue, as it can bring up feelings of fairness, jealousy, or resentment. To navigate this, it can be helpful to have clear criteria for distribution, to involve family members in the decision-making process, and to communicate openly and honestly about your decisions.

Family dynamics play a significant role in the process of Swedish Death Cleaning. By managing these dynamics through open communication, involvement, boundary-setting, and fair distribution, we can facilitate the process and enhance the outcomes of our decluttering efforts.

4. Dealing with Large American Homes

In the context of Swedish Death Cleaning, one of the unique challenges faced by many Americans is the size of their homes. American homes are often larger than their European counterparts, with more rooms, more storage space, and consequently, more belongings. This can make the process of decluttering seem daunting. However, with the right approach and mindset, dealing with large American homes can be effectively managed.

The first step in dealing with large homes is to change our perspective. Instead of viewing the size of the home as a challenge, we can see it as an opportunity. A larger home means more space to curate, more opportunities to create a living environment that truly reflects our values, passions, and lifestyle. It's an opportunity to create different spaces for different purposes, to experiment with different styles, and to create a home that is truly ours.

However, a larger home also means more potential for clutter. To prevent this, it's important to adopt a mindset of intentional ownership. This means consciously choosing what to bring into our homes, ensuring that each item serves a purpose or brings joy. It means resisting the urge to fill every space, and instead leaving room for movement, growth, and new possibilities.

When it comes to the actual process of decluttering, a large home can be tackled by breaking it down into smaller, more manageable tasks. Instead of trying to declutter the entire home at once, focus on one room or even one drawer at a time. This makes the task less overwhelming and allows for a sense of accomplishment with each completed task.

In a large home, it can be helpful to establish zones for different types of items. This not only makes it easier to find things, but also makes it easier to keep track of what you own. It can prevent the accumulation of duplicate items and make it easier to notice when things are starting to get cluttered.

Another strategy for dealing with large homes is to use the 'one in, one out' rule. This means that for every new item that comes into the home, an old one must leave. This helps maintain a balance of items and prevents the accumulation of clutter.

Involving family members in the process can also be beneficial in a large home. Each person can be responsible for decluttering their own space, and family decluttering days can be organized for common areas. This not only divides the task, but also promotes a sense of collective responsibility and ownership over the home.

Dealing with large American homes in the context of Swedish Death Cleaning involves changing our perspective, adopting a mindset of intentional ownership, breaking the task down into manageable parts, establishing zones, using the 'one in, one out' rule, and involving family members. By adopting these strategies, we can create a home that is not just large in size, but also large in value, joy, and purpose.

Swedish Death Cleaning is not about downsizing, but about right-sizing. It's about creating a home that fits our lifestyle, our needs, and our aspirations. And that includes dealing with the unique challenges and opportunities presented by large American homes. So, as we continue on this journey, let's embrace the size of our homes and use it as an opportunity to create a living environment that truly reflects who we are and what we value.

5. Setting New Household Habits

Swedish Death Cleaning is not a one-time event, but rather a lifelong practice. It's about setting new household habits that support a clutter-free, mindful, and intentional lifestyle. These habits are the foundation of a successful decluttering journey, ensuring that our homes remain a reflection of our values, passions, and legacy.

One of the key habits to establish is regular decluttering. This doesn't necessarily mean a full-house purge every few months. Instead, it could be as simple as a quick weekly check to remove any items that no longer serve a purpose or bring joy. It could also involve a more thorough decluttering of a specific area each month. The goal is to keep the clutter from accumulating and becoming overwhelming.

Another important habit is mindful consumption. This involves being conscious of what we bring into our homes, ensuring that each item serves a purpose or brings joy. It means resisting impulsive purchases and instead taking the time to consider whether an item truly aligns with our values and lifestyle.

In addition to these, it's also crucial to establish habits that support organization and cleanliness. This could involve setting a specific place for each item, making sure items are returned to their place after use, and regularly cleaning each area of the home. These habits not only maintain a clutter-free environment but also create a sense of peace and order.

Involving family members in these habits can also be beneficial. Each person can take responsibility for maintaining their own space, and family cleaning days can be organized for common areas. This not only divides the task but also promotes a sense of collective responsibility and ownership over the home.

It's important to remember that habits take time to establish. It's okay to start small, to make mistakes, and to adjust as needed. The goal is not perfection, but progress. Each small step towards a clutter-free, mindful, and intentional lifestyle is a victory worth celebrating.

Setting new household habits is a crucial part of our Swedish Death Cleaning journey. By establishing habits of regular decluttering, mindful consumption, organization, cleanliness, and family involvement, we can create a home that not only reflects our values, passions, and legacy, but also supports a peaceful, joyful, and fulfilling lifestyle.

Chapter 3

PLANNING FOR THE FUTURE

1. Legacy Planning Through Decluttering

One of the most profound aspects of Swedish Death Cleaning is its focus on legacy planning. This is not just about organizing our belongings; it's about curating a physical and emotional legacy for our loved ones. It's about ensuring that our belongings tell the story we want to be remembered by, and that they serve as a source of comfort, not a burden, for our loved ones after we're gone.

Legacy planning through decluttering involves several key steps. The first is to reassess our belongings with a focus on their emotional value, not just their practical value. This involves asking questions like: What memories or emotions does this item evoke? How does it reflect my values, my passions, or my identity? Would it bring joy or comfort to my loved ones?

This process can be emotional, as it involves revisiting memories and confronting our mortality. However, it can also be deeply rewarding. It allows us to reconnect with our past, to celebrate our journey, and to express our identity in a tangible way. It also allows us to create a meaningful legacy for our loved ones, one that reflects our love, our values, and our unique life story.

The next step in legacy planning is to decide what to do with our belongings. This could involve gifting certain items to loved ones, donating items to charities, selling items, or recycling them. The goal is to ensure that each item has a place and a purpose, and that our belongings as a whole reflect our values and our legacy.

Legacy planning also involves documenting our wishes for our belongings. This could involve writing a will, creating a list of items and their intended recipients, or simply discussing our wishes with our loved ones. This not only ensures that our wishes are respected, but also reduces potential conflicts or burdens for our loved ones.

Legacy planning through decluttering is a powerful aspect of Swedish Death Cleaning. It allows us to curate a meaningful legacy for our loved ones, to express our identity in a tangible way, and to ensure that our belongings serve as a source of comfort, not a burden, after we're gone. It's a process that involves reassessing our belongings, deciding what to do with them, and documenting our wishes.

2. Creating a Will and Communicating Your Wishes

Creating a will and communicating your wishes is an essential part of planning for the future, and it aligns perfectly with the principles of Swedish Death Cleaning. It's about taking control of your legacy, reducing potential burdens for your loved ones, and ensuring that your wishes are respected.

A will is a legal document that outlines how you want your assets to be distributed after your death. It can include everything from your home and financial assets to your personal belongings. It's a way to ensure that your belongings go to the people or organizations that you choose, and it can help prevent conflicts or misunderstandings among your loved ones.

Creating a will involves several key steps. The first is to take inventory of your assets. This includes not only your financial assets, but also your personal belongings. As part of Swedish Death Cleaning, you may already have a good idea of what you own and what you want to do with it.

The next step is to decide who you want to inherit your assets. This could be family members, friends, or charities that you care about. It's important to be specific and clear in your choices, to avoid potential misunderstandings or conflicts.

Once you've decided on your assets and beneficiaries, it's time to write your will. This can be done with the help of a lawyer, or through online services. It's important to ensure that your will is legally valid, which usually involves having it signed and witnessed.

But creating a will is not enough; it's also important to communicate your wishes to your loved ones. This involves having open and honest conversations about your will, your assets, and your wishes for your belongings. It's a chance to explain your choices, to address any concerns or questions, and to ensure that your loved ones understand and respect your wishes.

Communicating your wishes also extends beyond your will. It involves expressing your wishes for your end-of-life care, your funeral or memorial service, and even your digital legacy. It's about ensuring that all aspects of your life and death reflect your values, your wishes, and your legacy.

Creating a will and communicating your wishes is a crucial part of Swedish Death Cleaning and planning for the future. It's about taking control of your legacy, reducing potential burdens for your loved ones, and ensuring that your wishes are respected. It's a process that involves taking inventory of your assets, deciding on your beneficiaries, writing your will, and communicating your wishes.

3. Sorting Important Documents and Digital Assets

In the journey of Swedish Death Cleaning, sorting important documents and digital assets is a crucial task. These items, while not physically cluttering our spaces, hold significant value and can become a burden for loved ones if not properly managed. They are also an integral part of our legacy, containing vital information and memories.

Important documents include things like wills, deeds, insurance policies, financial statements, medical records, and personal identification documents. These papers often hold crucial information that will be needed by your loved ones in the event of your passing. They might also contain historical or sentimental value, offering a glimpse into your life and experiences.

Digital assets, on the other hand, include things like digital photos, emails, social media accounts, blogs, digital music, eBooks, and online banking or investment accounts. These assets, while intangible, can hold immense sentimental or financial value. They are a part of your digital legacy, a reflection of your life in the digital age.

Sorting important documents involves gathering them all in one place, reviewing them for relevance and accuracy, and then organizing them in a way that makes them easily accessible. This might involve creating a filing system, using a safe or lockbox for particularly sensitive documents, or even digitizing them for easier storage and access. It's also important to destroy any outdated or unnecessary documents to prevent confusion or identity theft.

Sorting digital assets can be a bit more complex due to the nature of digital data. It involves not only organizing your digital files but also managing your online accounts. This can include consolidating accounts, updating or deleting old content, backing up important files, and setting up a digital estate plan. This plan should include a list of your accounts, login information, and instructions on how you want each account to be handled.

Once your documents and digital assets are sorted, it's important to communicate this information to your loved ones or executor. They should know where to find your important documents and how to access your digital assets. This can save them time and stress in an already difficult time.

Sorting important documents and digital assets is a crucial part of Swedish Death Cleaning. It's about ensuring that your important information is organized, accessible, and known to your loved ones. It's about taking control of your legacy, both physical and digital, and ensuring that it reflects your life, your values, and your wishes.

4. Eco-Friendly Decluttering and Giving Back

In the process of Swedish Death Cleaning, decluttering is not just about removing items from our homes; it's about considering the impact of our belongings on the world around us. Eco-friendly decluttering and giving back are integral parts of this journey, reflecting our responsibility to our environment and our community.

Eco-friendly decluttering involves considering the lifecycle of our belongings and making decisions that minimize harm to the environment. This could involve choosing to recycle or compost items instead of sending them to the landfill, or opting to repair or repurpose items instead of replacing them. It's about recognizing that every item has an environmental footprint, and striving to make that footprint as small as possible.

Giving back, on the other hand, involves considering the social impact of our belongings. This could involve donating items to charities or individuals who can use them, or selling items and using the proceeds to support causes we care about. It's about recognizing that our belongings have value beyond our homes, and using that value to contribute to our community.

One of the first steps in eco-friendly decluttering is to assess the potential second life of our belongings. This involves considering whether items can be reused, repaired, repurposed, or recycled. It's about viewing our belongings not as waste, but as resources with potential value.

Next, we can seek out recycling programs, repair shops, and creative repurposing ideas. Many communities have resources available to help residents recycle or repurpose a wide variety of items, from electronics to clothing to furniture. Online platforms can also provide inspiration and guidance for repurposing items.

When it comes to giving back, we can start by identifying local charities or community groups that accept donations. These might include thrift stores, shelters, schools, or community centers. We can also consider selling items and donating the proceeds to a cause we care about.

In both eco-friendly decluttering and giving back, it's important to be mindful and intentional. This means taking the time to research and choose the best options, rather than simply choosing the easiest or most convenient. It also means respecting the value of our belongings and the impact they have on the world around us.

Eco-friendly decluttering and giving back are powerful ways to enhance our Swedish Death Cleaning journey. They allow us to minimize our environmental impact, contribute to our community, and add a deeper layer of meaning to our decluttering efforts.

5. Creating a Vision for the Future

Creating a vision for the future is the culmination of the Swedish Death Cleaning process. It's about looking beyond the decluttering, the sorting, the planning, and envisioning the life you want to lead. It's about creating a future that reflects your values, your passions, and your legacy.

This vision is not just about the physical space you inhabit, but also the emotional and mental space. It's about imagining a life that is unburdened by clutter, where every item in your home serves a purpose or brings joy. It's about envisioning a future where your loved ones are not burdened by your belongings, but instead find comfort and connection in them.

Creating a vision for the future also involves imagining the impact you want to have on the world. This might involve giving back to your community, contributing to causes you care about, or leaving a positive environmental legacy. It's about envisioning a future where your actions align with your values, and you can look back on your life with pride and satisfaction.

To create this vision, start by reflecting on your values, your passions, and your dreams. What kind of life do you want to lead? What kind of legacy do you want to leave? How do you want to be remembered?

Next, consider how your home and belongings fit into this vision. What changes do you need to make to align your physical space with your vision? How can you curate your belongings to reflect your values and passions?

Finally, consider the steps you need to take to realize this vision. This might involve further decluttering, reorganizing your space, or making lifestyle changes. It might involve creating a will, planning for your digital legacy, or setting new household habits.

Creating a vision for the future is a powerful part of the Swedish Death Cleaning process. It's about looking beyond the clutter and envisioning a future that reflects your values, your passions, and your legacy. It's about making intentional choices and taking deliberate steps towards that future.

Chapter 4

DECLUTTERING ROOM BY ROOM

1. Creating a Decluttering Plan for the Entire Home

Creating a decluttering plan for the entire home is the first step in the room-by-room Swedish Death Cleaning process. This plan serves as a roadmap, guiding us through each space and ensuring that we approach the process in a systematic, thoughtful, and effective way.

The first step in creating a decluttering plan is to assess each room in your home. This involves walking through your home and noting the state of each room. How cluttered is it? What types of items are in the room? How does the room make you feel? This assessment will give you a clear picture of the task ahead and help you prioritize your efforts.

Next, it's time to set goals for each room. These goals should reflect your overall vision for your home and your life. For example, you might want your kitchen to be a functional, clutter-free space where you can enjoy cooking. Or, you might want your bedroom to be a peaceful sanctuary, free from distractions and unnecessary items.

Once you have your goals, you can start to plan your approach for each room. This might involve deciding on a decluttering method, such as the box method or the four-box method. It might also involve deciding on a sequence for decluttering, such as starting with the easiest room to build momentum, or tackling the most cluttered room first for a big impact.

Your plan should also include strategies for dealing with different types of items. For example, you might decide to donate clothing and books, recycle old papers and electronics, and sell valuable items that you no longer need. You might also decide to involve family members in the process, assigning each person a room or a category of items.

Finally, your plan should include a schedule. Decluttering is a big task, and it can be overwhelming if you try to do it all at once. Instead, break the task down into manageable chunks and spread them out over time. This could involve dedicating a few hours each weekend to decluttering, or decluttering one room per month.

Creating a decluttering plan for the entire home is a crucial first step in the room-by-room Swedish Death Cleaning process. It provides a roadmap for the journey, helping us approach the task in a systematic, thoughtful, and effective way. It involves assessing each room, setting goals, planning our approach, and scheduling our efforts.

2. Decluttering the Kitchen

The kitchen, often referred to as the heart of the home, is a great place to continue our Swedish Death Cleaning journey. It's a space that is often filled with both practical items and sentimental items, from everyday dishes and appliances to heirloom china and holiday decorations.

The first step in decluttering the kitchen is to take inventory of what you have. This involves emptying out cupboards and drawers, sorting items into categories, and taking a hard look at what you own. How many dishes, pots, and pans do you have? How many gadgets and appliances? How many items are duplicates, or rarely used?

Once you have a clear picture of what you own, it's time to start making decisions. This involves asking the tough questions that are at the heart of Swedish Death Cleaning. Do you need this item? Do you use it regularly? Does it bring you joy? Does it have sentimental value? And importantly, would someone else be burdened by this item if you were to pass away?

As you make these decisions, remember to consider both the practical and emotional value of items. A rarely-used roasting pan might still be worth keeping if it's essential for your annual holiday dinner. An old set of dishes might be worth passing on to a loved one if it holds sentimental value.

Next, consider the best way to dispose of items you're getting rid of. Can they be sold, donated, recycled, or should they be thrown away? Remember the principles of eco-friendly decluttering and aim to minimize waste wherever possible.

Once you've decluttered, it's time to organize the remaining items in a way that makes sense for your lifestyle. This might involve rearranging cupboards, using organizers to maximize space, or even adding new storage solutions. The goal is to create a kitchen that is functional, enjoyable to use, and easy to keep clean.

Finally, consider how you can maintain a clutter-free kitchen in the future. This might involve setting new habits, such as cleaning up after each meal, putting things away immediately, or doing a quick decluttering session each season. It might also involve being more mindful about what you bring into the kitchen in the future.

Decluttering the kitchen is a significant step in the Swedish Death Cleaning process. It's a task that involves taking inventory, making decisions, disposing of items responsibly, organizing the remaining items, and setting new habits. It's a chance to create a kitchen that is not just clutter-free, but also a joy to use.

3. Tackling the Living Room and Family Spaces

The living room and family spaces are central to our homes and our lives. They are where we gather to relax, to connect, to entertain. They are filled with items that reflect our tastes, our interests, and our memories. As such, decluttering these spaces can be a significant task in the Swedish Death Cleaning process.

Start by taking inventory of the room. Remove all items from shelves, cupboards, and drawers, and group them into categories. This could include books, DVDs, games, decorative items, and electronics. As you sort, take note of how many items you have in each category and consider how often you use or enjoy them.

Next, begin the process of deciding what to keep and what to let go. Ask yourself the key questions of Swedish Death Cleaning: Do I need this? Do I use it? Does it bring me joy? Would it be a burden to others when I'm gone? Be honest with yourself, and remember that it's okay to let go of items, even if they hold sentimental value.

When deciding what to do with items you're letting go of, consider your options. Can they be sold, donated, or recycled? Could they be a blessing to someone else? Make a plan for each item, and follow through promptly to prevent second-guessing or the accumulation of clutter.

Once you've decluttered, it's time to organize the remaining items. Consider how you use the room and arrange your belongings to support those activities. For example, if your family enjoys movie nights, make sure your DVDs, remote controls, and blankets are easily accessible. If you love to read, create a cozy reading nook with your favorite books at hand.

Finally, think about how you can maintain a clutter-free living room in the future. This might involve regular decluttering sessions, new rules about what can be brought into the room, or habits to keep the room tidy. Remember, Swedish Death Cleaning is not a one-time event, but a lifelong practice.

Tackling the living room and family spaces is a significant part of the Swedish Death Cleaning process. It's about creating spaces that are not just clutter-free, but that support and enhance our lives. It's about making room for connection, relaxation, and joy.

4. Mastering Bedroom Decluttering

The bedroom, our personal sanctuary, is a space that often holds a mix of practical items and sentimental keepsakes. From clothing and accessories to books, photos, and mementos, each item in our bedroom can carry a weight of memories and emotions. As such, decluttering the bedroom can be a deeply personal and transformative part of the Swedish Death Cleaning process.

Begin by taking a comprehensive inventory of your bedroom. This involves removing all items from closets, drawers, and shelves, and grouping them into categories. As you sort, consider how often you use or enjoy each item. How many items do you have in each category? Are there items you've forgotten about or haven't used in a long time?

The next step is to decide what to keep and what to let go. This is where the principles of Swedish Death Cleaning come into play. Ask yourself: Do I need this item? Do I use it? Does it bring me joy? Would it be a burden to others when I'm gone? Be honest with yourself, and remember that it's okay to let go of items, even if they hold sentimental value.

When deciding what to do with items you're letting go of, consider your options. Can they be sold, donated, or recycled? Could they be a blessing to someone else? Make a plan for each item, and follow through promptly to prevent second-guessing or the accumulation of clutter.

Once you've decluttered, it's time to organize the remaining items. Consider how you use your bedroom and arrange your belongings to support those activities. For example, if you enjoy reading before bed, make sure your favorite books are within easy reach. If you get ready for the day in your bedroom, organize your clothing and accessories so they're easy to find and put away.

Finally, think about how you can maintain a clutter-free bedroom in the future. This might involve regular decluttering sessions, new rules about what can be brought into the room, or habits to keep the room tidy. Remember, Swedish Death Cleaning is not a one-time event, but a lifelong practice.

Mastering bedroom decluttering is a significant part of the Swedish Death Cleaning process. It's about creating a space that is not just clutter-free, but that supports and enhances our daily routines and our well-being. It's about making room for rest, relaxation, and personal expression.

5. Bathroom and Linen Closet Decluttering

The bathroom and linen closet, while often smaller spaces, can be a challenge to declutter. They tend to be home to many small items, from toiletries and cosmetics to towels and bed linens. These items can easily accumulate over time, leading to cluttered drawers, overflowing cabinets, and a lack of functional space. However, with the principles of Swedish Death Cleaning, we can transform these areas into organized, efficient, and pleasing spaces.

Start by taking inventory of the items in your bathroom and linen closet. This involves emptying out all cabinets, drawers, and shelves, and grouping items into categories. As you sort, take note of how many items you have in each category, and consider how often you use or need each item.

The next step is to decide what to keep and what to let go. This involves asking the key questions of Swedish Death Cleaning: Do I need this item? Do I use it? Does it bring me joy? Would it be a burden to others when I'm gone? Be honest with yourself, and remember that it's okay to let go of items, even if they're still usable or in good condition.

When deciding what to do with items you're letting go of, consider your options. Many toiletries and cosmetics can be recycled, and towels and linens can often be donated. Make a plan for each item, and follow through promptly to prevent second-guessing or the accumulation of clutter.

Once you've decluttered, it's time to organize the remaining items. Consider how you use your bathroom and linen closet, and arrange your belongings to support those activities. For example, you might keep everyday toiletries within easy reach, while storing extra supplies or less frequently used items in higher or deeper cabinets. Similarly, you might organize your linens by size or type, making it easy to find what you need.

Finally, think about how you can maintain a clutter-free bathroom and linen closet in the future. This might involve regular decluttering sessions, new rules about what can be brought into these spaces, or habits to keep these areas tidy. Remember, Swedish Death Cleaning is not a one-time event, but a lifelong practice.

Decluttering the bathroom and linen closet is a crucial part of the Swedish Death Cleaning process. It's about creating spaces that are not just clutter-free, but that support our daily routines and our well-being. It's about making room for cleanliness, efficiency, and ease.

Chapter 5

SENTIMENTAL ITEMS AND HEIRLOOMS

1. Understanding the Sentimental Value of Belongings

In the process of Swedish Death Cleaning, there's a particular category of items that often poses the greatest challenge: those with sentimental value. These are the belongings that tug at our heartstrings, that transport us back to another time, that remind us of people, places, and moments that we hold dear. They are the items that we keep not because we need them, but because we love them.

Understanding the sentimental value of belongings is a crucial part of the Swedish Death Cleaning process. It's about recognizing that our belongings are not just physical objects, but vessels for our memories, our emotions, and our identities. They are the tangible reminders of our past, the keepsakes of our experiences, the symbols of our relationships.

However, understanding the sentimental value of belongings is not about clinging to every item that holds a memory. It's about discerning which items truly enrich our lives and which ones are merely occupying space. It's about recognizing that our memories and emotions are not in the items themselves, but in us. The items are simply triggers for those memories and emotions.

This understanding can be liberating. It can free us from the burden of keeping every keepsake, every memento, every gift. It can empower us to let go of items that no longer serve us, even if they hold sentimental value. It can help us to declutter our homes and our lives, without feeling like we're discarding our past.

When evaluating the sentimental value of belongings, ask yourself: Does this item bring me joy? Does it remind me of a happy time, a loved one, a special event? Do I love to see it, touch it, use it? Or does it simply sit in a box, in a drawer, on a shelf, gathering dust?

Also, consider whether the item has a place in your future. Does it align with your vision for your life and your home? Does it fit with your current lifestyle and tastes? Can you imagine it being part of your life for many years to come?

Understanding the sentimental value of belongings is not about making black-and-white decisions. It's about making thoughtful, considered choices that honor your past, respect your present, and anticipate your future. It's about creating a home that reflects not just who you were, but who you are and who you aspire to be.

Understanding the sentimental value of belongings is a crucial part of the Swedish Death Cleaning process. It's about recognizing the emotional weight of our belongings, and making thoughtful, considered decisions about what to keep and what to let go. It's about creating a home and a life that reflect our values, our passions, and our legacy. So, as we continue on this journey, let's embrace the power of understanding and use it to transform our homes and our lives.

2. Dealing with Family Heirlooms

Family heirlooms can be some of the most challenging items to address in the Swedish Death Cleaning process. These are the items that have been passed down through generations, that carry the weight of our family history and heritage. They are often beautiful, valuable, and steeped in memories and emotions.

The first step in dealing with family heirlooms is to recognize their importance. These items are not just belongings; they are links to our past, tangible pieces of our family's story. They remind us of where we came from, of the people and events that shaped our family and, in turn, shaped us.

However, it's also important to recognize that the value of family heirlooms is not solely in their physical presence. The true value lies in the stories they tell, the memories they hold, the connections they represent. And these things can be preserved and honored even if the physical item is let go.

When deciding what to do with family heirlooms, consider your current lifestyle and your future plans. Do these items fit with your vision for your home and your life? Do they bring you joy, or do they feel more like a burden? Are you holding onto them out of obligation, or because you genuinely love and appreciate them?

If you choose to keep family heirlooms, make sure they have a place in your home. Display them proudly, use them regularly, or store them carefully. Treat them with the respect and care they deserve.

If you choose to let go of family heirlooms, consider how you can do so in a way that honors their significance. This might involve passing them on to other family members, donating them to a museum or historical society, or selling them to someone who will appreciate their value.

Dealing with family heirlooms is not about discarding your family's history. It's about choosing how you want to carry that history forward. It's about creating a home and a life that honor your past, respect your present, and anticipate your future.

Dealing with family heirlooms is a significant part of the Swedish Death Cleaning process. It's about recognizing the importance of these items, making thoughtful decisions about what to keep and what to let go, and finding ways to honor your family's history in a way that aligns with your current lifestyle and future plans. So, as we continue on this journey, let's embrace the power of choice and use it to transform our homes and our lives.

3. Managing Childhood and Memory Items

Childhood and memory items hold a unique place in our hearts. They are the tangible reminders of our past, the keepsakes of our experiences, the symbols of our personal history. They are the items that we keep not because we need them, but because they are part of our story. However, in the process of Swedish Death Cleaning, it's important to manage these items in a way that honors our past without cluttering our present or future.

Begin by taking a comprehensive inventory of your childhood and memory items. This may include toys, school projects, awards, letters, photos, and other mementos. As you sort through these items, take the time to reminisce and reflect. Each item is a piece of your story, a part of your journey.

Next, consider the value and significance of each item. Does it bring you joy? Does it remind you of a happy time, a loved one, a special event? Do you love to see it, touch it, remember it? Or does it simply sit in a box, in a drawer, on a shelf, gathering dust?

Also, consider whether the item has a place in your future. Does it align with your vision for your life and your home? Does it fit with your current lifestyle and tastes? Can you imagine it being part of your life for many years to come?

Once you've evaluated your items, decide what to keep and what to let go. Remember, it's okay to let go of items, even if they hold sentimental value. The memories are in you, not in the items. You can honor your past without holding onto every physical reminder of it.

When you let go of childhood and memory items, consider doing so in a way that honors their significance. This might involve passing them on to other family members, donating them to a museum or historical society, or recycling them in a respectful way.

If you choose to keep certain items, find a way to incorporate them into your home and your life. Display them, use them, enjoy them.

Don't let them languish in a box or a drawer. Let them be a part of your story that is alive and evolving.

Consider how you can manage your childhood and memory items in the future. This might involve regular decluttering sessions, creating a special place for memory items, or setting limits on what you keep.

Managing childhood and memory items is a significant part of the Swedish Death Cleaning process. It's about honoring your past, making thoughtful decisions about what to keep and what to let go, and finding ways to incorporate your memories into your current lifestyle and future plans. So, as we continue on this journey, let's embrace the power of memory and use it to transform our homes and our lives.

4. Preserving Memories in Meaningful Ways

One of the most beautiful aspects of Swedish Death Cleaning is that it's not just about letting go; it's also about preserving memories in meaningful ways. It's about finding ways to honor our past, our experiences, and our loved ones, without cluttering our homes and our lives.

One way to preserve memories is through photos. Instead of keeping boxes of old photos, consider creating digital albums or printing a select few to display in your home. This not only reduces physical clutter but also allows you to enjoy these memories regularly.

Another way to preserve memories is through storytelling. Write down your memories, your stories, your experiences. This could be in the form of a journal, a memoir, or letters to your loved ones. Sharing your stories not only preserves your memories but also allows you to pass on your wisdom, your lessons, and your legacy.

You can also preserve memories by repurposing items. For example, you might turn a loved one's shirt into a cushion cover, or a collection of postcards into a piece of wall art. This allows you to keep the item in a way that is functional and visible, rather than hidden away in a box.

In addition, consider creating a memory box. This is a special box where you keep a select few items that hold significant sentimental value. The key is to be selective, choosing only those items that truly bring you joy and that you wish to carry with you into your future.

When preserving memories, it's important to remember that it's the memory, not the item, that is important. You don't need to keep every item from your past to honor your memories. Instead, choose to preserve your memories in ways that align with your current lifestyle and future plans, and that bring you joy and satisfaction.

Preserving memories in meaningful ways is a significant part of the Swedish Death Cleaning process. It's about honoring your past, your experiences, and your loved ones, without cluttering your home and your life. It's about finding creative, satisfying ways to keep your memories alive, while also making space for your present and your future.

5. Involving Loved Ones in Decisions

Involving loved ones in the process of Swedish Death Cleaning can be a deeply meaningful and rewarding experience. It not only helps to share the workload but also provides an opportunity for connection, communication, and shared understanding.

When you involve your loved ones in decisions about sentimental items and heirlooms, you give them a voice in the process. You allow them to express their feelings, their memories, and their desires. This can lead to deeper conversations, stronger bonds, and a shared sense of history and legacy.

Involving loved ones in decisions can also help to alleviate any potential guilt or pressure you may feel about letting go of certain items. If a loved one expresses a desire to keep an item, you can pass it on to them with peace of mind, knowing it will be cherished. If they agree that an item can be let go, you can do so with their support and understanding.

However, it's important to approach these conversations with sensitivity and respect. Remember that your loved ones may have different feelings, memories, and attachments to these items. They may need time to process, to reminisce, and to decide. Be patient, be open, and be willing to listen.

Involving loved ones in decisions is not just about getting their input or approval. It's about sharing the journey, the memories, and the decisions. It's about coming together as a family, as a team, to honor the past, respect the present, and anticipate the future.

Involving loved ones in decisions is a significant part of the Swedish Death Cleaning process. It's about sharing the journey, the memories, and the decisions. It's about strengthening relationships, deepening understanding, and creating a shared legacy. So, as we continue on this journey, let's embrace the power of connection and use it to transform our homes and our lives.

Chapter 6

DIGITAL DECLUTTERING

1. Why Digital Clutter Matters

In our modern, digital age, clutter is not confined to physical spaces. It also extends to our digital lives. Emails, files, photos, apps, and social media accounts can all accumulate over time, leading to a sense of digital clutter. Just as physical clutter can impact our well-being and productivity, so too can digital clutter.

Digital clutter matters because it can lead to feelings of overwhelm and stress. When your digital spaces are disorganized and overflowing, it can be difficult to find the information you need. You may waste time searching for files, or feel stressed by the sheer volume of unread emails in your inbox. This can lead to frustration, inefficiency, and a sense of being out of control.

Moreover, digital clutter can distract us from our priorities and goals. Every unnecessary app notification, every irrelevant email, every unneeded file takes our attention away from what truly matters. This constant barrage of digital information can lead to a scattered mind, making it difficult to focus and concentrate.

Digital clutter can also impact our privacy and security. Unorganized digital spaces can make it harder to protect sensitive information, increasing the risk of data breaches and identity theft. It's crucial to manage and organize our digital data to safeguard our personal information.

Furthermore, digital clutter can be a burden for our loved ones after we're gone. Just as we don't want to leave a physical mess for others to clean up, we also don't want to leave a digital mess. By decluttering our digital lives, we can ensure that our digital legacy is as tidy and organized as our physical one.

In the context of Swedish Death Cleaning, addressing digital clutter is an extension of the principles of decluttering and simplifying. It's about creating digital spaces that are organized, efficient, and manageable. It's about ensuring that our digital lives support, rather than hinder, our overall well-being and productivity.

Digital clutter matters because it impacts our efficiency, our focus, our privacy, and our legacy. By addressing digital clutter, we can create digital spaces that support our well-being, our productivity, and our peace of mind. As we continue on this journey of Swedish Death Cleaning, let's remember to extend our decluttering efforts to our digital lives as well.

2. Organizing Digital Photos and Files

In the realm of digital clutter, photos and files often represent the most significant challenge. These are the digital equivalents of the boxes of photos and stacks of papers that accumulate in our physical spaces. They can quickly become overwhelming if not properly managed. However, with a thoughtful approach, you can organize your digital photos and files in a way that makes them manageable, accessible, and enjoyable.

Start by taking a comprehensive inventory of your digital photos and files. This might involve going through your computer's hard drive, your smartphone, your tablet, and any other digital devices you use. It might also involve checking cloud storage services, social media platforms, and email accounts.

As you go through your digital photos and files, start to categorize them. You might create folders for different types of files, such as work documents, personal documents, family photos, vacation photos, and so on. You might also create subfolders for different years, events, or projects.

Next, start to declutter. Just as with physical items, ask yourself: Does this file or photo bring me joy? Does it serve a purpose? Is it something I want to keep for the future? If not, it's time to let it go. This might involve deleting unnecessary files or photos, or it might involve transferring them to an external hard drive or cloud storage service for safekeeping.

Once you've decluttered, it's time to organize. This might involve renaming files or photos to make them easier to find, or it might involve arranging them in a way that makes sense to you. The key is to create a system that is intuitive and manageable, so you can easily locate and enjoy your digital photos and files.

Finally, consider how you can maintain this organization in the future. This might involve regular decluttering sessions, or it might involve creating habits that prevent digital clutter from accumulating in the first place. For example, you might make it a habit to delete unnecessary files or photos as soon as you're done with them, or to immediately file away new documents in their appropriate folder.

Organizing digital photos and files is a significant part of managing digital clutter. It's about creating digital spaces that are efficient, manageable, and enjoyable. It's about ensuring that our digital lives support our well-being, our productivity, and our peace of mind. As we continue on this journey of Swedish Death Cleaning, let's remember to extend our decluttering and organizing efforts to our digital lives as well.

3. Decluttering Your Social Media and Email

In our interconnected world, social media and email are integral parts of our daily lives. They allow us to communicate, connect, and share with others. However, they can also become sources of digital clutter that can lead to feelings of overwhelm and stress. Just as we declutter our physical and digital spaces, it's important to declutter our social media and email.

Begin with your social media accounts. These platforms can quickly become cluttered with unnecessary posts, photos, and connections. Start by going through your friends or followers list. Are there people you no longer interact with or who no longer bring positivity to your life? It's okay to unfollow or unfriend them. This is not about being rude or unkind; it's about curating a social media environment that brings you joy and supports your well-being.

Next, look at the content you're consuming on social media. Are there pages, groups, or accounts that you follow that don't align with your interests or values? Do they clutter your feed with posts that don't interest or inspire you? Don't hesitate to unfollow these accounts. Remember, your social media feed should be a source of inspiration, connection, and positivity, not stress or negativity.

Now, let's move on to email. If your inbox is overflowing with unread messages, it's time for a declutter. Start by deleting or archiving old emails that you no longer need. Then, tackle your unread emails. If an email is not important or relevant, delete it. If it requires a response, respond as soon as possible and then archive it.

Next, look at your email subscriptions. Are there newsletters, updates, or promotions that you no longer read or find useful? Unsubscribe from these emails. This will significantly reduce the number of emails coming into your inbox, making it more manageable and less cluttered.

Finally, consider setting up folders or labels in your email to organize your messages. This can make it easier to find important emails and keep your inbox tidy. You might have folders for different categories like work, personal, bills, or travel.

Maintaining a decluttered social media and email requires ongoing effort. Regularly review your friends or followers list, the accounts you follow, and your email subscriptions. Set aside time each week to manage your emails, deleting or archiving old messages and organizing new ones.

Decluttering your social media and email is an important part of managing digital clutter. It's about curating a digital environment that supports your well-being, productivity, and peace of mind. It's about taking control of the content you consume and the messages you receive. As we continue on this journey of Swedish Death Cleaning, let's remember to extend our decluttering efforts to our social media and email, creating digital spaces that bring us joy, connection, and inspiration.

4. Safeguarding Important Digital Documents

While decluttering our digital lives is crucial, it's equally important to safeguard important digital documents. These documents might include financial records, legal documents, personal identification, and other sensitive information. In our digital age, these documents often exist in digital form, and it's essential to protect them from loss, damage, or unauthorized access.

Start by identifying your important digital documents. These might include tax returns, bank statements, contracts, insurance policies, medical records, passports, or birth certificates. It's a good idea to create a list of these documents for easy reference.

Once you've identified your important documents, make sure they're stored securely. This might involve saving them on your computer's hard drive, on an external hard drive, or in a cloud storage service. If you're storing documents on your computer or an external hard drive, make sure these devices are protected with a strong, unique password.

Next, consider creating backups of your important documents. This can provide an extra layer of protection in case your original files are lost or damaged. You might back up your files to an external hard drive, a cloud storage service, or a secure online backup service. Remember to regularly update your backups to ensure they include the most recent versions of your documents.

In addition to storing and backing up your documents, it's important to protect them from unauthorized access. This might involve encrypting your files, using a secure network connection, and regularly updating your software and devices to protect against security threats. Be wary of phishing scams or other attempts to gain access to your personal information.

Finally, as part of your Swedish Death Cleaning process, consider your digital legacy. What will happen to your digital documents when you're gone? You might consider creating a digital will or a plan for your digital assets. This could involve appointing a digital executor, sharing your passwords with a trusted individual, or using a digital legacy service.

Safeguarding important digital documents is a crucial part of managing digital clutter. It's about protecting your personal information, your financial records, and your digital legacy. It's about ensuring that your digital life is not only decluttered but also secure and prepared for the future. As we continue on this journey of Swedish Death Cleaning, let's remember to extend our decluttering efforts to include the safeguarding of our important digital documents.

5. Maintaining a Clean Digital Life

Just like maintaining a clutter-free physical environment, maintaining a clean digital life requires ongoing effort and commitment. It's not a one-time task, but rather a continuous process of evaluation, organization, and mindful consumption. The goal is to create a digital environment that supports your well-being, productivity, and peace of mind.

Start by establishing regular decluttering sessions. Just as you might set aside time each week to tidy your home, set aside time to tidy your digital spaces. This might involve deleting unnecessary files, organizing your documents, managing your emails, or reviewing your social media feeds. Regular maintenance can prevent digital clutter from accumulating and becoming overwhelming.

Next, consider your digital consumption habits. Are you mindlessly downloading apps, subscribing to newsletters, or following social media accounts that don't add value to your life? Be mindful of what you're bringing into your digital space. Just as you would think twice before bringing a new item into your home, think twice before adding to your digital clutter.

Also, consider setting boundaries for your digital life. This might involve setting specific times for checking email or social media, turning off unnecessary notifications, or taking regular digital detoxes. Boundaries can help you maintain control over your digital life, rather than feeling controlled by it.

In addition, make use of tools and features that can help you maintain a clean digital life. Many devices and platforms offer organization, storage, and security features that can help you manage your digital clutter. For example, you might use folders, labels, or tags to organize your files and emails, or you might use a password manager to securely store your passwords.

Remember that maintaining a clean digital life is not about achieving perfection. It's about creating a digital environment that supports your lifestyle, your goals, and your well-being. It's okay if your digital spaces aren't perfectly organized or completely clutter-free. What matters is that they're manageable, functional, and aligned with your needs and values.

Maintaining a clean digital life is a crucial part of managing digital clutter. It's about regular maintenance, mindful consumption, and thoughtful organization. It's about creating a digital environment that supports your well-being, productivity, and peace of mind. As we continue on this journey of Swedish Death Cleaning, let's remember to extend our decluttering efforts to our digital lives, creating digital spaces that bring us joy, connection, and inspiration.

Chapter 7

MINIMALISM FOR THE SOUL

1. The Emotional Liberation of Decluttering

The journey of Swedish Death Cleaning is not just about the physical act of decluttering. It's also about the emotional liberation that comes with letting go. Decluttering can be a deeply emotional process, stirring up memories, feelings, and attachments. But it can also be a profoundly liberating one, freeing us from the weight of unnecessary possessions and opening up space for new experiences, emotions, and opportunities.

When we hold onto physical items, we often hold onto the emotions associated with them. These might be positive emotions, like joy, love, or nostalgia. But they can also be negative emotions, like guilt, regret, or sadness. Over time, these emotions can accumulate, creating a kind of emotional clutter that weighs us down.

Decluttering allows us to confront and release these emotions. It gives us the opportunity to revisit our past, to honor our memories, and to process our feelings. It allows us to let go of the items and the emotions that no longer serve us, freeing us from their weight.

The emotional liberation of decluttering is not always easy. It can be challenging to let go of items that hold sentimental value or that are associated with important people or events in our lives. But it's important to remember that letting go of an item doesn't mean letting go of the memory or the person associated with it.

In fact, decluttering can actually enhance our memories and relationships. When we're surrounded by too many items, it can be difficult to appreciate any of them fully. But when we declutter, we can focus on the items that truly matter to us, that truly bring us joy and evoke meaningful memories. We can honor these items and the memories and people associated with them more fully.

Furthermore, decluttering can free up emotional energy. When we're not weighed down by unnecessary possessions and the emotions associated with them, we have more energy to focus on the present and the future. We have more energy to invest in our relationships, our passions, and our growth.

The emotional liberation of decluttering is a powerful aspect of the Swedish Death Cleaning process. It's about confronting and releasing emotional clutter, honoring our memories and relationships, and freeing up emotional energy. It's about creating a physical and emotional environment that supports our well-being, our growth, and our peace of mind. As we continue on this journey, let's embrace the emotional liberation of decluttering and the freedom, clarity, and joy it can bring.

2. How Minimalism Enhances Well-Being

Minimalism, at its core, is about stripping away the unnecessary to make room for what truly matters. It's about choosing quality over quantity, and value over volume. In the context of Swedish Death Cleaning, minimalism is a guiding principle that can significantly enhance our well-being.

Firstly, minimalism can reduce stress. A cluttered environment can be a constant source of low-level stress, subtly draining our energy and attention. By contrast, a minimalist environment is calming and restful. It allows us to relax, focus, and breathe more easily. When we're not surrounded by unnecessary items, we're not constantly reminded of tasks to be done or decisions to be made. We're free to simply be.

Secondly, minimalism can save time and energy. When we own fewer items, we spend less time cleaning, organizing, repairing, and managing them. This frees up time and energy for activities that bring us joy and fulfillment. It allows us to invest in our relationships, our passions, and our personal growth.

Thirdly, minimalism can enhance our sense of control and competence. When our environment is orderly and manageable, we feel more in control of our lives. We feel capable and competent, which boosts our self-esteem and self-efficacy. This sense of control can extend to other areas of our lives, improving our overall well-being.

Fourthly, minimalism can promote mindful consumption. When we adopt a minimalist mindset, we become more intentional about what we bring into our lives. We consider the value and purpose of each item, rather than mindlessly accumulating possessions. This mindful consumption can extend to other areas of our lives, such as our diet, our media consumption, and our use of resources.

Finally, minimalism can foster gratitude and contentment. When we're not constantly seeking more, we can appreciate what we already have. We can find joy and fulfillment in the simple, everyday things. We can cultivate a sense of contentment that isn't dependent on possessions or acquisitions.

Minimalism is a powerful tool for enhancing well-being. It reduces stress, saves time and energy, enhances control and competence, promotes mindful consumption, and fosters gratitude and contentment. As we continue on this journey of Swedish Death Cleaning, let's embrace the principles of minimalism and the many benefits they can bring to our lives. Let's create spaces and lives that reflect our values, our priorities, and our true selves.

3. Creating Emotional Space for Personal Growth

The process of decluttering and adopting a minimalist lifestyle does more than just create physical space. It also creates emotional space, which can be a powerful catalyst for personal growth. When we clear out the unnecessary, whether it's physical items or emotional baggage, we make room for new experiences, feelings, and insights. This emotional space can be a fertile ground for personal growth and transformation.

When our lives are cluttered with unnecessary possessions, we often feel weighed down, overwhelmed, and stuck. Our energy is consumed by managing our stuff, leaving little room for anything else. Our minds are constantly distracted by the chaos around us, making it difficult to focus on our goals, dreams, and passions. We may feel like we're simply surviving, rather than truly living.

By decluttering and embracing minimalism, we can free up this emotional energy. We can shift our focus from managing our stuff to exploring our interests, developing our skills, and nurturing our relationships. We can invest our energy in activities that bring us joy, fulfillment, and a sense of purpose. We can start to live more intentionally, aligning our actions with our values and aspirations.

Creating emotional space also allows us to better understand ourselves. When we're not distracted by clutter, we can tune into our thoughts, feelings, and desires more easily. We can reflect on our experiences, learn from our mistakes, and gain insights into our patterns and behaviors. This self-awareness is a key component of personal growth, helping us to change unhelpful habits, develop new skills, and become more authentic and fulfilled individuals.

Furthermore, creating emotional space can enhance our resilience and adaptability. When we're not weighed down by unnecessary possessions or emotional baggage, we're better able to cope with life's challenges and changes. We can navigate transitions more smoothly, adapt to new situations more quickly, and bounce back from setbacks more easily. We can become more flexible and resilient, which can greatly enhance our overall well-being and quality of life.

Creating emotional space can also open us up to new opportunities. When we're not tied down by clutter, we're more open to new experiences, relationships, and ideas. We can take risks, pursue opportunities, and explore new paths. We can grow, evolve, and transform in ways we might never have imagined.

Creating emotional space through decluttering and minimalism is a powerful way to foster personal growth. It frees up emotional energy, enhances self-awareness, boosts resilience and adaptability, and opens up new opportunities. As we continue on this journey of Swedish Death Cleaning, let's remember to create not just physical space, but also emotional space. Let's make room for growth, transformation, and the full expression of our true selves.

4. Letting Go of Mental Clutter

Just as our physical spaces can become cluttered with unnecessary items, so too can our minds become cluttered with unnecessary thoughts, worries, and mental tasks. This mental clutter can be just as draining and overwhelming as physical clutter, if not more so. It can distract us, stress us out, and prevent us from focusing on what truly matters. As part of our journey towards minimalism and emotional liberation, it's important to address not just our physical clutter, but our mental clutter as well.

The process of letting go of mental clutter involves becoming aware of our thoughts and mental tasks, evaluating their usefulness and impact, and consciously choosing to let go of those that are unnecessary or unhelpful. This can be a challenging process, as our minds are often busy and our thoughts can be persistent. However, with practice and patience, we can learn to manage our mental clutter and create a more peaceful, focused mind.

Begin by simply observing your thoughts. Without trying to change or judge them, just notice what's going on in your mind. You might notice worries about the future, regrets about the past, self-critical thoughts, or endless to-do lists. These are all forms of mental clutter.

Once you've become aware of your mental clutter, start to evaluate it. Are these thoughts helpful? Do they serve a purpose? Are they based on reality? Often, you'll find that much of your mental clutter consists of unnecessary worries, unrealistic expectations, or unhelpful self-criticism.

Next, start to let go of this mental clutter. This might involve challenging unrealistic thoughts, letting go of things you can't control, or practicing self-compassion. It might involve delegating tasks, setting boundaries, or simplifying your schedule. It might involve mindfulness practices, such as meditation or deep breathing, which can help to calm your mind and reduce mental clutter.

Remember, letting go of mental clutter is not about achieving a completely empty mind. Rather, it's about creating space in your mind for the thoughts, feelings, and experiences that truly matter. It's about reducing the noise so you can hear the music.

Letting go of mental clutter can have a profound impact on your well-being. It can reduce stress, enhance focus, boost mood, and improve sleep. It can free up mental energy for creativity, problem-solving, and decision-making. It can help you to be more present, mindful, and engaged in your life.

Letting go of mental clutter is a crucial part of the journey towards minimalism and emotional liberation. It's about creating a more peaceful, focused, and intentional mind. It's about making space for the thoughts, feelings, and experiences that truly matter. As we continue on this journey of Swedish Death Cleaning, let's remember to declutter not just our physical spaces, but our mental spaces as well. Let's create minds that are clear, focused, and free.

5. Mindfulness and Decluttering

Mindfulness is a powerful tool that can support and enhance the process of decluttering. At its core, mindfulness is about being fully present and engaged in the current moment. It's about observing our thoughts, feelings, and experiences without judgment. When applied to decluttering, mindfulness can help us make more intentional decisions, manage our emotions, and find joy and fulfillment in the process.

When we declutter mindfully, we pay attention to each item we're sorting through. We notice its physical characteristics, its purpose, and the feelings it evokes in us. We consider whether it adds value to our lives, whether it brings us joy, and whether it aligns with our current needs and values. This mindful attention can help us make more intentional decisions about what to keep and what to let go of.

Mindfulness can also help us manage the emotions that often arise during decluttering. It can help us stay calm and centered, even when we're dealing with difficult decisions or strong emotions. It can help us observe our feelings without getting swept up in them, allowing us to process them in a healthy, constructive way.

Furthermore, mindfulness can help us find joy and fulfillment in the process of decluttering. Instead of rushing through it as a chore to be completed, we can approach it as an opportunity to engage fully with our lives. We can appreciate the physical act of sorting through our items, the memories and experiences they evoke, and the sense of space and clarity that comes from letting go.

Mindfulness and decluttering go hand in hand. Mindfulness enhances the process of decluttering, while decluttering creates the physical and mental space for more mindful living. As we continue on this journey of Swedish Death Cleaning, let's remember to bring mindfulness into our decluttering efforts. Let's engage fully with the process, manage our emotions with compassion, and find joy and fulfillment in each moment.

Chapter 8

ECO-FRIENDLY DECLUTTERING

1. Sustainable Decluttering Practices

It's essential to consider the environmental impact of our decluttering efforts. While it's important to clear our homes of unnecessary items, it's equally important to dispose of these items responsibly. Sustainable decluttering practices can help us minimize waste, reduce our carbon footprint, and contribute to a healthier planet.

Sustainable decluttering involves considering the entire lifecycle of our belongings. When we decide to let go of an item, we should think about where it will end up. Will it go to a landfill, where it will contribute to pollution and waste? Or can it be reused, recycled, or composted, reducing its environmental impact?

One sustainable decluttering practice is to donate items that are still in good condition. This not only keeps these items out of landfills but also gives them a new life. Donated items can be used by others, reducing the need for new items to be produced. When donating items, consider local charities, thrift stores, or community organizations. You might also consider online platforms that facilitate the exchange of used goods.

Another sustainable decluttering practice is to recycle items that can't be reused. Many items, from paper and cardboard to electronics and appliances, can be recycled. Recycling these items can save resources and reduce pollution. However, it's important to recycle responsibly. Not all items can be recycled in your regular household recycling bin. Some items, like electronics or hazardous materials, need to be recycled through special programs or facilities.

Composting is another sustainable decluttering practice. Organic waste, like food scraps or yard waste, can be composted at home, turning waste into nutrient-rich soil. Composting not only reduces the amount of waste going to landfills but also enriches your garden, reduces the need for chemical fertilizers, and helps combat climate change by reducing greenhouse gas emissions.

Finally, sustainable decluttering involves being mindful of what we bring into our homes in the first place. By choosing items that are durable, reusable, and made from sustainable materials, we can reduce the need for future decluttering. We can also support companies and industries that prioritize sustainability.

Sustainable decluttering is an essential part of Swedish Death Cleaning. It's about taking responsibility for our belongings, from the moment we acquire them to the moment we let them go. It's about reducing waste, supporting sustainability, and contributing to a healthier planet. As we continue on this journey, let's strive to make our decluttering efforts as sustainable as possible.

2. Donation vs. Recycling

When we declutter our homes, we're often left with a pile of items that we no longer need or want. The question then becomes: what should we do with these items? Two of the most eco-friendly options are donation and recycling. Both of these options can keep items out of landfills, reduce waste, and conserve resources. However, they each have their own benefits and considerations.

Donation is a great option for items that are still in good condition and can be used by others. This might include clothing, furniture, appliances, books, toys, and more. When we donate these items, we give them a new life and prevent the need for new items to be produced. We also support charities and community organizations, many of which rely on donated goods to fund their programs and services.

However, it's important to donate responsibly. Not all items are suitable for donation, and not all charities can accept all types of items. Before donating, consider the condition of the item and the needs of the organization. If an item is broken, stained, or otherwise unusable, it might be better to recycle it. If an organization doesn't need or can't accept a certain type of item, it might be better to find another organization that can.

Recycling is another eco-friendly option for decluttering. Recycling involves breaking down items into their raw materials, which can then be used to produce new items. This can save resources, reduce pollution, and conserve energy. Many items can be recycled, including paper, plastic, metal, glass, electronics, and more.

However, like donation, recycling requires some consideration. Not all items can be recycled, and not all recycling programs accept all types of items. Some items, like electronics or hazardous materials, need to be recycled through special programs or facilities. It's also important to recycle items correctly, as incorrect recycling can contaminate recycling streams and make the recycling process less efficient.

Both donation and recycling are valuable tools in our eco-friendly decluttering toolkit. They allow us to dispose of our unwanted items responsibly, reducing waste and supporting sustainability. As we continue on our journey of Swedish Death Cleaning, let's consider both of these options and choose the one that's most appropriate for each item. Let's strive to make our decluttering efforts not just good for us, but good for the planet as well.

3. Responsible Disposal of Household Items

5692As we embark on the journey of Swedish Death Cleaning, we inevitably encounter items that can neither be donated nor recycled. These might include broken appliances, worn-out furniture, or outdated electronics. While it might be tempting to simply throw these items in the trash, responsible disposal is crucial for minimizing our environmental impact.

One of the most responsible ways to dispose of household items is through special waste disposal programs. Many cities and towns offer these programs, which allow residents to safely dispose of items that can't be handled through regular trash or recycling services. These might include electronics, batteries, light bulbs, paint, chemicals, and other potentially hazardous materials. These programs ensure that these items are disposed of safely, preventing them from ending up in landfills or contaminating the environment.

For large items like furniture or appliances, consider special pick-up services. Many waste management companies offer bulk pick-up services, which can handle large items that can't be disposed of through regular trash services. Some companies even offer white goods recycling, which can safely recycle appliances like refrigerators, stoves, and washing machines.

Another option for responsible disposal is to repurpose items. With a bit of creativity and effort, many items can be given a new life. Old furniture can be refurbished or upcycled into new pieces. Broken electronics can be taken apart and their components used for other projects. Even worn-out clothing can be repurposed into rags, quilts, or stuffing for pillows or pet beds.

For items that can't be donated, recycled, or repurposed, the most responsible disposal option might be the landfill. However, it's important to minimize the amount of waste we send to landfills. Landfills are a major source of greenhouse gas emissions, and they can also contaminate soil and water. Before sending an item to the landfill, consider all other options and make sure that there's truly no other way to dispose of it.

Responsible disposal of household items is an essential part of eco-friendly decluttering. It involves considering all options, from special disposal programs to repurposing, and choosing the one that minimizes environmental impact. As we continue on our journey of

Swedish Death Cleaning, let's strive to dispose of our unwanted items in the most responsible, eco-friendly way possible. Let's make our decluttering efforts not just good for us, but good for the planet as well.

4. Choosing Eco-Friendly Alternatives

As we embrace the principles of Swedish Death Cleaning and declutter our homes, we're also presented with an opportunity to rethink our consumption habits. The items we choose to bring into our homes after decluttering can have a significant impact on our environment. By choosing eco-friendly alternatives, we can reduce our carbon footprint, conserve resources, and contribute to a more sustainable world.

Eco-friendly alternatives are products that are designed with the environment in mind. They are typically made from sustainable materials, produced using energy-efficient processes, and packaged with minimal and recyclable materials. They are durable, reusable, and often biodegradable. They are products that do good for us and for the planet.

When choosing eco-friendly alternatives, consider the materials the product is made from. Look for products made from natural, renewable, and recycled materials. Avoid products made from non-renewable resources, such as petroleum-based plastics. Also, consider the durability of the product. A product that lasts longer can be more eco-friendly, as it reduces the need for replacement and waste.

Consider the energy used in the production and transportation of the product. Products that are locally made or made using renewable energy are often more eco-friendly. Also, consider the packaging of the product. Look for minimal packaging, and packaging that can be recycled or composted.

In addition to choosing eco-friendly products, consider reducing your consumption overall. The most eco-friendly product is the one you don't buy. By buying less and choosing only what you truly need, you can reduce waste and save resources.

Consider also the end life of the product. Can it be recycled or composted? Can it be repaired or repurposed? A product that can be disposed of responsibly is a more eco-friendly choice.

Choosing eco-friendly alternatives is not just about buying green products. It's also about adopting a green mindset. It's about considering the environmental impact of our choices and striving to make choices that are good for the planet. It's about recognizing our role as consumers and using our purchasing power to support sustainable practices.

Choosing eco-friendly alternatives is a powerful way to make our decluttering efforts more sustainable. It's about making conscious, mindful choices that reflect our values and our commitment to the planet. As we continue on our journey of Swedish Death Cleaning, let's strive to choose eco-friendly alternatives and create homes that are not just clutter-free, but also eco-friendly.

5. Making Decluttering Part of an Eco-Conscious Lifestyle

The process of decluttering, when done thoughtfully and responsibly, naturally aligns with an eco-conscious lifestyle. It's about being mindful of what we own, why we own it, and how it impacts our lives and the world around us. It's about reducing waste, conserving resources, and making choices that reflect our values and our commitment to the planet.

Making decluttering part of an eco-conscious lifestyle involves more than just disposing of items responsibly. It also involves rethinking our consumption habits. It involves choosing quality over quantity, and value over convenience. It involves choosing items that are made from sustainable materials, produced in an ethical manner, and designed to last. It involves repairing, repurposing, and reusing items, rather than discarding them at the first sign of wear or damage.

An eco-conscious lifestyle also involves being mindful of our energy use. This can be as simple as turning off lights when we leave a room, unplugging electronics when they're not in use, or choosing energy-efficient appliances. It can also involve larger changes, like installing solar panels, insulating our homes, or choosing a green energy provider.

Furthermore, an eco-conscious lifestyle involves considering the broader impact of our choices. It involves supporting companies and industries that prioritize sustainability. It involves advocating for policies and practices that protect the environment. It involves educating ourselves and others about the importance of sustainability.

Making decluttering part of an eco-conscious lifestyle is a natural and powerful step. It's about aligning our actions with our values, and creating homes and lives that reflect our commitment to the planet. As we continue on our journey of Swedish Death Cleaning, let's strive to make decluttering not just a one-time event, but a lifelong practice that contributes to a more sustainable world.

Chapter 9

INVOLVING YOUR FAMILY IN SWEDISH DEATH CLEANING

1. How to Have Open Conversations

Swedish Death Cleaning is a deeply personal process, but it's also one that can greatly benefit from the involvement and support of family members. However, initiating conversations about decluttering, especially when it's tied to end-of-life planning, can be challenging. It's a sensitive topic that can bring up a range of emotions. Yet, open conversations are crucial for ensuring everyone understands the process and its benefits.

The first step to having open conversations about Swedish Death Cleaning is to approach the topic with sensitivity and respect. It's important to acknowledge that the process might bring up strong emotions, including fear, sadness, or resistance. Be patient, listen actively, and validate these feelings. Remember that it's not just about getting rid of stuff; it's about dealing with memories, attachments, and the reality of our mortality.

When explaining the concept of Swedish Death Cleaning, focus on its benefits. Highlight how it can create a more peaceful, organized living environment. Explain how it can ease the burden on loved ones in the future. Share how it can provide an opportunity to reminisce and celebrate life. Make it clear that it's not about erasing memories, but about honoring them in a way that respects both the past and the future.

Encourage family members to ask questions and express their concerns. This is not a monologue, but a dialogue. Their input is valuable and can provide different perspectives on the process. They may also have practical suggestions or offer to help in ways you hadn't considered.

When discussing specific items, be open about your reasons for wanting to let go of them. If an item holds significant sentimental value for a family member, consider offering it to them or finding a way to preserve its memory that doesn't involve physical storage, such as photographing it.

Be patient and persistent. It may take several conversations before your family members fully understand and support the process. Don't rush them or pressure them into accepting it immediately. Instead, give them time to process the information and come to terms with it.

Having open conversations about Swedish Death Cleaning is a crucial step in involving your family in the process. It's about sharing your intentions, addressing concerns, and working together towards a common goal. It's about fostering understanding, support, and cooperation. As we continue on this journey, let's remember the importance of open, respectful, and patient communication.

2. Teaching Children the Value of Less

In a world that often equates more with better, teaching children the value of less can be a challenging yet rewarding endeavor. Swedish Death Cleaning, with its emphasis on mindful ownership and intentional living, provides an excellent framework for these lessons. It's an opportunity to instill values of simplicity, sustainability, and gratitude in the younger generation.

Start by explaining the concept of Swedish Death Cleaning in age-appropriate terms. For younger children, you might talk about it as a way of making room for what's truly important. For older children, you can delve into deeper discussions about consumerism, waste, and the impact of our choices on the environment.

Demonstrate the value of less through your own actions. Let your children see you decluttering, organizing, and making mindful decisions about what to keep and what to let go of. Show them that you value quality over quantity, and that you can find joy and satisfaction in simplicity.

Involve your children in the decluttering process. This can be as simple as asking them to sort through their toys and choose which ones to keep and which ones to donate. Make sure to respect their choices and their pace. Remember that decluttering can be emotional, even for children.

Use decluttering as an opportunity to discuss the life cycle of items. Talk about where things come from, how they're made, and what happens to them when we're done with them. Discuss the concept of waste and the importance of recycling and reusing.

Encourage your children to think critically about their possessions. Ask them questions like: Do you use this? Do you love it? Does it add value to your life? Teach them to consider these questions before acquiring new items.

Teach your children about the joy of giving. Encourage them to donate their unwanted items to those in need. Explain how their old toys can bring joy to other children, and how their old clothes can keep someone warm.

Cultivate an attitude of gratitude in your home. Encourage your children to appreciate what they have, rather than longing for what they don't have. Teach them to take care of their possessions and to value the memories and experiences associated with them.

Teaching children the value of less is a valuable lesson that can benefit them throughout their lives. It can help them resist the pressures of consumerism, make mindful decisions, and find joy in simplicity. As we continue on our journey of Swedish Death Cleaning, let's remember to involve our children and pass on these valuable lessons to the next generation.

3. Creating Family Decluttering Projects

Involving your family in the process of Swedish Death Cleaning can transform what might seem like a daunting task into a meaningful and bonding experience. Creating family decluttering projects is a practical way to engage everyone in the process, fostering cooperation, shared responsibility, and mutual understanding.

One way to create a family decluttering project is to focus on a specific area of the house. This could be a communal space like the living room or kitchen, or a clutter hotspot like the garage or basement. The key is to choose an area that everyone uses and can contribute to decluttering. Start by assessing the area together, discussing what works and what doesn't, and deciding what needs to go.

Next, divide the tasks among family members according to their abilities and interests. For example, younger children can sort through toys or books, while teenagers might be responsible for electronics or clothing. Adults can handle more complex tasks like paperwork or sentimental items. Everyone should have a role, and everyone's contribution should be valued.

As you work on the project, encourage open communication. Allow space for discussions about why certain items are being kept or let go. This can lead to deeper conversations about values, memories, and the meaning of possessions. It can also help family members understand and respect each other's perspectives.

Make sure to celebrate progress along the way. Decluttering can be hard work, both physically and emotionally, and it's important to acknowledge everyone's efforts. This could be as simple as a word of praise or as elaborate as a family outing or special meal. The goal is to create positive associations with the decluttering process.

Once the project is complete, reflect on the experience together. What did you learn? How has the space improved? How does it feel to have less clutter? Use these reflections to motivate future decluttering projects and to reinforce the principles of Swedish Death Cleaning.

Moving forward, consider making family decluttering projects a regular event. This could be once a month, once a season, or whenever you feel clutter starting to accumulate. Regular decluttering can prevent clutter from building up and can keep the principles of Swedish Death Cleaning fresh in everyone's minds.

Finally, remember that the goal of these projects is not just to declutter, but to bring your family together. It's about working towards a common goal, understanding each other better, and creating a home that reflects your shared values and aspirations. It's about creating not just a clutter-free home, but a closer, more harmonious family.

Creating family decluttering projects is a practical and meaningful way to involve your family in Swedish Death Cleaning. It's about cooperation, communication, and shared responsibility. It's about transforming the task of decluttering into an opportunity for family bonding and personal growth. As we continue on our journey of Swedish Death Cleaning, let's remember to involve our families, share the experience, and make decluttering a family affair.

4. Handling Resistance from Family Members

As you embark on the journey of Swedish Death Cleaning, you might encounter resistance from some family members. This resistance can come in many forms, from outright refusal to subtle avoidance, and it can stem from various sources, including fear, misunderstanding, or emotional attachment. Handling this resistance requires patience, empathy, and open communication.

Firstly, it's important to understand the reasons behind the resistance. Is it fear of change or loss? Is it misunderstanding or lack of knowledge about Swedish Death Cleaning? Is it emotional attachment to possessions? Or is it simply resistance to the idea of decluttering? Understanding the root cause can help you address the resistance effectively.

If the resistance is due to fear, reassure your family members that Swedish Death Cleaning is not about erasing memories or preparing for the end. Instead, it's about simplifying life, reducing stress, and making room for what truly matters. It's about creating a peaceful, organized home that reflects who you are and what you value.

If the resistance is due to misunderstanding, take the time to explain the concept of Swedish Death Cleaning. Share its benefits, its purpose, and its process. Highlight that it's a gradual, mindful process, not a drastic, one-time event. Also, share your personal reasons for embracing Swedish Death Cleaning and how you hope it will benefit the family.

If the resistance is due to emotional attachment, be sensitive and understanding. Respect their feelings and give them space to process their emotions. Encourage them to express their feelings and share their memories. Remember that it's not just about getting rid of stuff, but about dealing with memories and attachments.

If the resistance is simply to the idea of decluttering, try to find common ground. Maybe they're not ready for Swedish Death Cleaning, but they're open to organizing or cleaning. Start with these smaller tasks and gradually introduce the principles of Swedish Death Cleaning.

In all cases, be patient and persistent. Change can be difficult, especially when it involves letting go of possessions. Don't rush your family members or pressure them into accepting Swedish Death Cleaning. Instead, give them time to understand and accept the concept. Keep the lines of communication open and continue to share your experiences and insights.

Handling resistance from family members is a common challenge in the process of Swedish Death Cleaning. It requires understanding, patience, and open communication. It's about respecting each other's feelings and perspectives, finding common ground, and working together towards a shared goal. As we continue on our journey of Swedish Death Cleaning, let's remember to handle resistance with empathy and patience, and to keep our focus on the benefits and purpose of this transformative process.

5. Making Swedish Death Cleaning a Family Tradition

Incorporating Swedish Death Cleaning into your family traditions can be a powerful way to maintain a clutter-free home and pass on the values of simplicity, mindfulness, and intentional living to future generations. Making it a family tradition can help normalize the process, making it a regular part of your family's life and fostering a collective commitment to a clutter-free, intentional lifestyle.

Start by establishing regular decluttering sessions. These could be timed with seasonal changes, holidays, or family milestones. Make these sessions a family event, involving everyone in the process. This not only divides the work but also fosters a sense of shared responsibility and cooperation.

During these sessions, encourage open discussions about the items being decluttered. Share stories, reminisce about the past, and reflect on the memories associated with the items. This can make the process more meaningful and enjoyable, turning it from a chore into a cherished family activity.

In addition to decluttering, incorporate other aspects of Swedish Death Cleaning into your family traditions. This could include mindful shopping practices, sustainable living habits, or regular discussions about the value of less. The goal is to embed the principles of Swedish Death Cleaning into your family's lifestyle and values.

Celebrate the completion of each decluttering session. This could be a special meal, a family outing, or simply a relaxing evening together. Celebrations can help reinforce the positive associations with Swedish Death Cleaning and motivate everyone for future sessions.

Remember to be flexible and adaptable. As your family grows and changes, your Swedish Death Cleaning traditions should evolve as well. What works for your family now might not work in the future. Be open to changes and always seek ways to make the process enjoyable and meaningful for everyone.

Making Swedish Death Cleaning a family tradition is a powerful way to maintain a clutter-free home and pass on valuable life principles. It's about fostering a collective commitment to simplicity, mindfulness, and intentional living. As we continue on our journey of Swedish Death Cleaning, let's remember to make it a part of our family traditions, embedding it into our family's lifestyle and values, and passing it on to future generations.

Chapter 10

DECLUTTERING BEYOND THE HOME

1. Decluttering Your Office Space

Swedish Death Cleaning, while often associated with decluttering our homes, can also be applied to other areas of our lives. One such area is our office space. Whether you work in a corporate office, a home office, or a shared workspace, decluttering can create a more productive, efficient, and peaceful work environment.

The first step in decluttering your office space is to assess your current situation. Look around your workspace. Are there piles of papers on your desk? Are your drawers filled with unused stationery? Are your digital files disorganized and hard to locate? Acknowledging the current state of your office is the first step towards creating a more organized and efficient workspace.

Next, start the decluttering process. Start with physical items. Go through your desk, drawers, and shelves. Dispose of any items that are broken or no longer needed. Recycle any papers that are no longer relevant. Donate any items that are still in good condition but no longer serve a purpose in your workspace.

When decluttering, ask yourself: Do I use this? Do I need this? Does this contribute to my productivity? If the answer is no, it's time to let it go. Remember, the goal is not to create an empty space, but a space that supports your work and enhances your productivity.

Once you've decluttered the physical items, turn your attention to your digital space. This includes your computer, email, and any other digital tools you use. Delete any files you no longer need. Organize your files into folders for easy access. Unsubscribe from any newsletters or email lists that no longer serve you.

After decluttering, organize your workspace. Create a system that works for you. This could involve using trays to organize papers, labeling drawers, or creating a filing system. The key is to create a system that makes it easy to find what you need when you need it.

Maintaining a decluttered office space is an ongoing process. Regularly review your space and declutter as needed. This could be once a week, once a month, or whenever you feel your space becoming cluttered.

Remember that a decluttered office space is not just about aesthetics. It's about creating a space that supports your work, enhances your productivity, and contributes to your overall well-being. It's about creating a space that reflects the principles of Swedish Death Cleaning: simplicity, mindfulness, and intentional living.

Decluttering your office space is a powerful way to enhance your work experience. It's about creating a space that supports your productivity, reduces stress, and reflects your values. As we continue on our journey of Swedish Death Cleaning, let's remember to extend the principles beyond our homes and into all areas of our lives, including our workspaces.

2. Organizing Storage Units

Storage units can often become a catch-all for items we're not quite ready to part with, but don't necessarily have a place for in our homes. Over time, these units can become cluttered, disorganized, and overwhelming. Applying the principles of Swedish Death Cleaning to our storage units can help us reclaim these spaces, making them functional and efficient.

The first step in organizing a storage unit is to take inventory. This involves going through the unit and making a list of what's inside. This can be a time-consuming process, but it's an essential step in understanding what you're dealing with. As you go through the items, you might be surprised at what you find. There might be items you forgot you had, items you no longer need, or items that are damaged or outdated.

Once you have a clear understanding of what's in your storage unit, start the decluttering process. Use the principles of Swedish Death Cleaning to guide you. Ask yourself: Do I need this? Do I use this? Does this item bring me joy or serve a purpose? If the answer is no, it's time to let it go. Remember, the goal is not to empty the storage unit, but to ensure that everything in it has a purpose and a place.

As you declutter, sort items into categories: keep, donate, sell, recycle, or trash. Be ruthless in your decluttering. If you haven't used an item in the past year, it's probably time to let it go. If an item is damaged or no longer functional, it's time to dispose of it responsibly.

After decluttering, it's time to organize the items you've decided to keep. Group similar items together. Use boxes, bins, or shelving to keep items organized and easy to find. Label everything clearly. The goal is to create a system that makes it easy to locate and access your items when you need them.

Maintaining an organized storage unit is an ongoing process. Regularly review the contents of your unit. As you acquire new items, make sure to declutter and organize as needed. This will prevent the unit from becoming cluttered and disorganized again.

Organizing a storage unit using the principles of Swedish Death Cleaning can help you reclaim your space, reduce stress, and make your life more organized and efficient. It's about making conscious decisions about what to keep and what to let go, and creating a space that serves your needs and reflects your values. As we continue on our journey of Swedish Death Cleaning, let's remember to extend these principles beyond our homes and into all areas of our lives, including our storage units.

3. Simplifying Your Car and Vehicles

Our vehicles, much like our homes, can easily become cluttered with unnecessary items. From old receipts and food wrappers to unused accessories and emergency supplies, the clutter can accumulate over time, creating a chaotic and stressful environment. Applying the principles of Swedish Death Cleaning to our vehicles can help us create a more organized, efficient, and enjoyable driving experience.

The first step in simplifying your car is to remove all the items and take inventory. This includes everything in the glove compartment, center console, door pockets, trunk, and any other storage areas. Lay everything out and assess what you truly need in your car. You might be surprised at the amount of unnecessary items that have accumulated over time.

Next, start the decluttering process. Use the principles of Swedish Death Cleaning to guide your decisions. Ask yourself: Do I need this item in my car? Do I use it regularly? Does it serve a purpose? If the answer is no, it's time to let it go. Remember, the goal is not to empty your car, but to ensure that everything in it serves a purpose and contributes to a pleasant driving experience.

As you declutter, sort items into categories: keep, donate, sell, recycle, or trash. Be ruthless in your decluttering. If an item has been in your car for months without being used, it's probably time to remove it. If an item is damaged or no longer functional, dispose of it responsibly.

After decluttering, it's time to organize the items you've decided to keep. Group similar items together and designate a specific place for each item. For example, keep all emergency supplies in a single, easily accessible location. Use organizers or storage containers to keep items neat and prevent them from moving around while driving.

Maintaining a clutter-free car is an ongoing process. Regularly review the contents of your car and declutter as needed. This could be once a week, once a month, or whenever you feel your car becoming cluttered. Regular decluttering will prevent clutter from building up and will keep your car organized and efficient.

Simplifying your car using the principles of Swedish Death Cleaning can enhance your driving experience, reduce stress, and create a more organized and efficient vehicle. It's about making conscious decisions about what to keep in your car and what to let go, and creating a space that serves your needs and reflects your values. As we continue on our journey of Swedish Death Cleaning, let's remember to extend these principles beyond our homes and into all areas of our lives, including our vehicles.

4. Minimalism in Travel and Leisure

The principles of Swedish Death Cleaning can also be applied to our travel and leisure activities. Embracing minimalism in these areas can enhance our experiences, reduce stress, and allow us to focus on the joy of the journey rather than the burden of our belongings.

When planning a trip, consider what you truly need to take with you. Many of us have a tendency to overpack, filling our suitcases with items "just in case" we need them. However, this often leads to heavy luggage, disorganization, and stress. Instead, aim to pack only what you know you will use. Choose versatile clothing items that can be mixed and matched, and limit the number of shoes and accessories. Remember, the goal is not to deprive yourself, but to free yourself from the burden of unnecessary items.

Similarly, when booking accommodations, consider what you truly need. Do you need a large hotel suite, or would a smaller, simpler room suffice? Do you need a rental car, or could you use public transportation or walk? By choosing simpler, less cluttered options, you can reduce stress and focus on the experiences rather than the possessions.

When it comes to leisure activities, consider the clutter that can come with hobbies. Do you have equipment or supplies for hobbies you no longer enjoy? Are you holding onto items out of guilt or obligation? If so, it might be time to let them go. Keep only what you truly use and enjoy, and give yourself permission to let go of the rest.

In addition to physical clutter, consider also the mental clutter that can come with travel and leisure. This might include over-planning, over-scheduling, or setting unrealistic expectations. Instead, aim to create space for spontaneity, relaxation, and enjoyment. Remember, the goal of travel and leisure is to create joyful experiences, not to check items off a list.

Maintaining minimalism in travel and leisure is an ongoing process. Regularly review your habits and make adjustments as needed. This could be before each trip, at the start of each season, or whenever you feel your travel or leisure activities becoming cluttered.

Embracing minimalism in travel and leisure can enhance our experiences, reduce stress, and allow us to focus on the joy of the journey. It's about making conscious decisions about what we truly need and want, and creating space for experiences rather than possessions. As we continue on our journey of Swedish Death Cleaning, let's remember to extend these principles beyond our homes and into all areas of our lives, including our travel and leisure activities.

5. Maintaining Order in Your Work-Life Balance

The principles of Swedish Death Cleaning can also be applied to maintaining order in your work-life balance. This balance is crucial for overall well-being, productivity, and satisfaction in both personal and professional life. However, just like physical spaces, our schedules and commitments can become cluttered and overwhelming.

Start by assessing your current work-life balance. Are you spending too much time at work and not enough on personal pursuits? Do you feel overwhelmed by your commitments? Are there activities or commitments that no longer serve you? Acknowledging the current state of your work-life balance is the first step towards creating a more balanced and fulfilling life.

Next, start the decluttering process. This involves letting go of unnecessary commitments, activities, and tasks. Ask yourself: Does this activity or commitment bring me joy or value? Does it contribute to my goals and well-being? If the answer is no, it's time to let it go. This might involve delegating tasks, saying no to new commitments, or stepping back from activities that no longer serve you.

Once you've decluttered your schedule, it's time to create a balance that supports your well-being and goals. This might involve setting boundaries around work, making time for relaxation and self-care, and prioritizing activities that bring you joy and fulfillment. Remember, the goal is not to create an empty schedule, but a balanced and fulfilling one.

Maintaining a balanced work-life schedule is an ongoing process. Regularly review your schedule and make adjustments as needed. This could be once a week, once a month, or whenever you feel your work-life balance becoming unbalanced. Regular reviews will prevent your schedule from becoming cluttered and will keep your work-life balance in check.

Maintaining order in your work-life balance using the principles of Swedish Death Cleaning can enhance your well-being, productivity, and satisfaction in both personal and professional life. It's about making conscious decisions about what to keep and what to let go, and creating a balance that serves your needs and reflects your values. As we continue on our journey of Swedish Death Cleaning, let's remember to extend these principles beyond our homes and into all areas of our lives, including our work-life balance.

Chapter 11

LIVING INTENTIONALLY POST-DECLUTTERING

1. Maintaining a Minimalist Lifestyle

Once you've decluttered your home, office, and other areas of your life, the journey of Swedish Death Cleaning doesn't end. In fact, it's just beginning. The next step is to maintain a minimalist lifestyle. This is not about living with the bare minimum, but rather making intentional choices about what you bring into your life and what you choose to let go.

Maintaining a minimalist lifestyle starts with mindfulness. Be conscious of the items you bring into your home and life. Before making a purchase, ask yourself: Do I need this? Will I use this? Does this item bring me joy or serve a purpose? If the answer is no, it's probably best to leave the item behind. This mindfulness can prevent unnecessary items from cluttering your space and life.

Next, regularly review your belongings. Even with mindful purchasing, it's natural for items to accumulate over time. Regularly reviewing your items can help you identify and remove any unnecessary items before they become clutter. This could be a monthly, seasonal, or annual review, depending on what works best for you.

In addition to physical items, consider also the activities and commitments in your life. Are there activities that no longer bring you joy or serve a purpose? Are there commitments that are more draining than fulfilling? If so, it might be time to let them go. Remember, minimalism is not just about physical clutter, but also mental and emotional clutter.

Embrace the simplicity and freedom that comes with a minimalist lifestyle. Without the burden of unnecessary items and commitments, you can focus on what truly matters to you. This could be spending time with loved ones, pursuing hobbies, or simply enjoying the peace and tranquility of a clutter-free home.

Maintaining a minimalist lifestyle is an ongoing journey of mindfulness, regular reviews, and intentional choices. It's about creating a life that reflects your values and brings you joy. As we continue on our journey of Swedish Death Cleaning, let's remember to extend these principles beyond the decluttering process and into our everyday lives. Let's embrace the simplicity, freedom, and joy of a minimalist lifestyle.

2. Setting Boundaries on New Purchases

One of the essential aspects of maintaining a minimalist lifestyle and a clutter-free home is setting boundaries on new purchases. This is where the principles of Swedish Death Cleaning can be truly transformative, shifting not just how we deal with existing clutter, but how we approach consumption in the first place.

Setting boundaries on new purchases starts with mindfulness. Before making a purchase, take a moment to consider why you are buying the item. Is it out of necessity, or is it an impulse buy? Does the item serve a specific purpose, or does it bring you joy? If not, it might be best to reconsider the purchase.

Next, consider the lifespan of the item. Will it be used regularly, or will it end up gathering dust after a few uses? Is it made to last, or will it need to be replaced in a short time? By considering the lifespan of an item before purchasing, you can avoid bringing temporary or disposable items into your home.

Another important boundary to set is on duplicate items. Do you already have a similar item at home? If so, is there a need for another one? Often, we buy items not because we need them, but because we like them. By setting a boundary against duplicates, you can significantly reduce the number of unnecessary items in your home.

Setting a budget can also be a helpful boundary. By allocating a specific amount for shopping, you can curb impulse buys and focus on purchasing items that are truly necessary or meaningful. Remember, the goal is not to deprive yourself, but to make intentional and mindful purchases.

Lastly, consider the storage space for the new item. Is there a designated spot for it in your home? If not, where will it be kept? If there's no proper storage space for it, the item might end up contributing to clutter.

Maintaining these boundaries requires ongoing commitment and mindfulness. It's not always easy, especially in a consumer-driven culture. However, by setting and respecting these boundaries, you can maintain a clutter-free home, reduce waste, save money, and lead a more minimalist and intentional lifestyle.

Setting boundaries on new purchases is a crucial step in living intentionally post-decluttering. It's about making mindful decisions, considering the lifespan of items, avoiding duplicates, setting a budget, and planning storage space. As we continue our journey of Swedish Death Cleaning, let's remember to extend these principles to our shopping habits. Let's embrace the freedom and simplicity that comes with mindful consumption.

3. Creating Habits for a Clutter-Free Life

Creating habits for a clutter-free life is a crucial part of living intentionally post-decluttering. These habits can help maintain the cleanliness and organization of your space, reduce stress, and enhance your overall well-being.

One of the most effective habits is regular decluttering. This doesn't mean you need to conduct a full-scale decluttering session every week. Instead, dedicate a few minutes each day to maintaining your space. This could be as simple as putting items back in their designated places after use, or spending a few minutes each day sorting through a particular area of your home.

Another beneficial habit is the "one in, one out" rule. This means that for every new item you bring into your home, you should remove an existing item. This habit can prevent the accumulation of new clutter and can help you maintain a minimalist lifestyle.

Practicing mindful shopping is also a crucial habit for a clutter-free life. Before making a purchase, take a moment to consider whether you truly need the item, whether it will add value to your life, and where it will be stored in your home. This habit can help you avoid impulse purchases and keep your home free from unnecessary items.

Creating a designated place for every item in your home is another effective habit. When every item has a home, it's easier to maintain order and prevent clutter from building up. If you find an item that doesn't have a designated place, it's a sign that you may need to reassess whether it's necessary.

Implementing a regular cleaning schedule can also help maintain a clutter-free home. This doesn't just mean cleaning in terms of hygiene, but also in terms of organization. Regularly tidying your space can prevent clutter from building up and can make your home more enjoyable to live in.

Lastly, practicing gratitude can be a powerful habit for a clutter-free life. By appreciating what you have, you can reduce the desire for new, unnecessary items. Regularly take time to appreciate your home and the items within it that serve you and bring you joy.

Creating habits for a clutter-free life is a key aspect of living intentionally post-decluttering. Regular decluttering, the "one in, one out" rule, mindful shopping, designated places for items, a regular cleaning schedule, and practicing gratitude are all effective habits that can help you maintain a clutter-free and joyful home. As we continue our journey of Swedish Death Cleaning, let's remember to incorporate these habits into our daily lives to sustain our clutter-free environments.

4. Finding Joy in Simplicity

Finding joy in simplicity is the heart of Swedish Death Cleaning and the minimalist lifestyle. It's about shifting our focus from the quantity of our possessions to the quality of our experiences. It's about appreciating the beauty in less, rather than more. It's about understanding that the most meaningful moments in life often come from the simplest things.

When we declutter our homes and our lives, we create space. Space not just in a physical sense, but also in a mental and emotional sense. We create room for new experiences, new ideas, and new growth. We free ourselves from the burden of unnecessary possessions and commitments, allowing us to focus on what truly matters.

Finding joy in simplicity means savoring the everyday moments. It's about enjoying a quiet morning with a cup of coffee, reading a book in a clutter-free living room, or having a meaningful conversation with a loved one without distractions. It's about appreciating the beauty of a well-organized home, where every item has a place and a purpose.

Finding joy in simplicity also means redefining success and fulfillment. In a society that often equates success with material wealth and busyness, choosing simplicity can be a radical act. It's about understanding that success is not about having more, but about being more. It's about finding fulfillment not in possessions, but in experiences and relationships.

Finding joy in simplicity is also about embracing mindfulness. It's about being present in the moment, rather than constantly striving for more. It's about appreciating what we have, rather than what we don't. It's about understanding that the most meaningful moments in life are often the simplest.

Maintaining a minimalist lifestyle and finding joy in simplicity is an ongoing journey. It requires mindfulness, intentionality, and sometimes, courage. It's not always easy, especially in a consumer-driven culture. However, the rewards are immense. A clutter-free home, a simpler life, and a focus on what truly matters can bring a sense of peace, fulfillment, and joy that material possessions can't.

Finding joy in simplicity is a key aspect of living intentionally post-decluttering. It's about savoring the everyday moments, redefining success, embracing mindfulness, and appreciating the beauty of a well-organized home. As we continue our journey of Swedish Death Cleaning, let's remember to find joy in the simplicity that a clutter-free life brings. Let's embrace the freedom, peace, and fulfillment that comes from living with less, and focus on the joy and beauty of the simple moments in life.

5. Continuing the Swedish Death Cleaning Journey

The Swedish Death Cleaning journey is not a one-time event, but a continuous process. It's a lifestyle choice that involves ongoing mindfulness, intentionality, and commitment. It's about continually reassessing our belongings, our commitments, and our lifestyle, and making adjustments as needed.

Continuing the Swedish Death Cleaning journey means regularly reviewing our possessions and letting go of items that no longer serve us. It's about being mindful of new purchases and only bringing items into our homes that add value or joy. It's about maintaining a clutter-free home, not just for our own peace and well-being, but also for the ease of our loved ones in the future.

Continuing the journey also means regularly reassessing our commitments and activities. Are there activities or commitments that no longer bring us joy or serve a purpose? Are we maintaining a healthy work-life balance? Are we making time for relaxation, self-care, and activities that bring us joy and fulfillment? Regularly reassessing and adjusting our commitments can help us maintain a balanced and fulfilling lifestyle.

Continuing the Swedish Death Cleaning journey is also about embracing the principles of minimalism and simplicity in all areas of our lives. It's about finding joy in the simple moments, appreciating what we have, and understanding that the most meaningful moments in life often come from the simplest things.

Continuing the Swedish Death Cleaning journey is about maintaining a clutter-free home and lifestyle, regularly reassessing our possessions and commitments, and embracing the principles of minimalism and simplicity. It's a journey that can bring peace, fulfillment, and joy. As we continue on this journey, let's remember to embrace the simplicity, freedom, and joy that a clutter-free life brings. Let's continue to make intentional choices, appreciate the simple moments, and find joy in the journey itself.

Chapter 12

PLANNING YOUR LEGACY

1. Communicating Your Final Wishes

The concept of Swedish Death Cleaning is deeply intertwined with the idea of legacy planning. It's not just about decluttering your physical space, but also about preparing for the future and easing the burden on your loved ones. A crucial part of this process is communicating your final wishes.

Communicating your final wishes is about having open, honest discussions with your loved ones about what you want to happen after your death. This can include your preferences for your funeral or memorial service, your wishes for your possessions, and your instructions for your financial assets. While these conversations can be difficult, they are crucial for ensuring that your wishes are respected and that your loved ones are not left with uncertainty or disputes.

Start by documenting your wishes. Write down your preferences for your funeral or memorial service, including any specific details you have in mind. This could include the type of service you want, the music or readings you prefer, and any other personal touches you'd like to include.

Next, consider your possessions. Which items would you like to pass on to specific people? Are there items with sentimental value that you'd like to keep within the family? Are there items that you'd like to donate to a specific cause? Documenting these wishes can help ensure that your possessions are distributed according to your preferences.

Your financial assets are another important aspect of your final wishes. This includes your savings, investments, real estate, and other assets. Consider seeking advice from a financial advisor or estate planning attorney to ensure that your assets are distributed in the most effective and tax-efficient way.

Once you've documented your final wishes, share them with your loved ones. This can be a difficult conversation, but it's an important one. Be open and honest about your wishes, and reassure your loved ones that these plans are about easing their burden and ensuring that your wishes are respected.

Communicating your final wishes is a crucial part of Swedish Death Cleaning and legacy planning. By documenting your wishes for your funeral, your possessions, and your financial assets, and sharing these wishes with your loved ones, you can ensure that your legacy is respected and that your loved ones are not left with unnecessary burdens. As we continue our journey of Swedish Death Cleaning, let's remember to consider not just the physical clutter in our lives, but also the emotional and practical aspects of our legacy.

2. Decluttering as Part of Estate Planning

Estate planning is a critical part of preparing for the future, and decluttering plays a significant role in this process. By decluttering, you can simplify the task of managing your estate and reduce the burden on your loved ones.

When we think of estate planning, we often think of legal and financial matters, such as creating a will or setting up a trust. However, estate planning also involves managing your physical possessions. This is where decluttering comes in. By reducing the number of items you own, you can make it easier for your loved ones to manage your estate.

Start by identifying the items that have monetary value. These could include real estate, vehicles, jewelry, artwork, antiques, or collectibles. You may want to have these items appraised and include them in your will or trust.

Next, consider the items that have sentimental value. These could include family heirlooms, photographs, letters, or other items that hold special meaning for you or your loved ones. You might want to pass these items on to specific family members or friends, or you might want to keep them within the family.

Once you've identified the items of monetary and sentimental value, it's time to declutter the rest. This might include clothing, furniture, kitchenware, books, and other everyday items. Consider donating these items to charity, selling them, or recycling them.

Decluttering as part of estate planning is not just about reducing the number of items you own. It's also about making intentional decisions about the items you choose to keep and the items you choose to let go. It's about considering the value and meaning of your possessions, and making choices that reflect your values and wishes.

Decluttering is a process, not a one-time event. It might take weeks, months, or even years, depending on the number of items you own and the pace at which you choose to declutter. Be patient with yourself, and remember that every item you remove is one less item for your loved ones to manage.

Decluttering is a critical part of estate planning. By reducing the number of items you own, you can simplify the task of managing your estate and reduce the burden on your loved ones. As we continue our journey of Swedish Death Cleaning, let's remember to consider not just the physical clutter in our lives, but also the practical aspects of our legacy. Let's make intentional decisions about our possessions, and create a legacy that reflects our values and wishes.

3. Leaving Behind a Clutter-Free Legacy

Leaving behind a clutter-free legacy is a profound act of love and consideration for your loved ones. It's about ensuring that the task of managing your estate is as straightforward and stress-free as possible. It's about respecting your loved ones' time and emotional well-being. It's about creating a legacy that reflects your values and the life you've lived.

A clutter-free legacy starts with decluttering. This involves going through your possessions and deciding what to keep, what to pass on, and what to let go. It's about making intentional decisions about your belongings and ensuring that each item in your home serves a purpose or brings you joy.

Leaving behind a clutter-free legacy also involves planning for your possessions. This could mean designating certain items to be passed on to specific family members or friends, or it could mean arranging for certain items to be sold or donated. It's about making your wishes known and ensuring that your possessions are handled in a way that aligns with your values.

Leaving behind a clutter-free legacy is not just about physical possessions, though. It's also about your digital footprint. In today's digital age, we all leave behind a trail of digital clutter, from social media accounts to digital photos to emails. As part of your clutter-free legacy, consider how you want your digital footprint to be managed. This could involve deleting unnecessary accounts, organizing digital files, or even designating a digital executor.

Leaving behind a clutter-free legacy is also about your financial affairs. This involves ensuring that your financial documents are organized and easily accessible, and that your loved ones are aware of your financial situation and wishes. This can greatly ease the burden on your loved ones and ensure that your financial affairs are handled in a way that aligns with your wishes.

Lastly, leaving behind a clutter-free legacy involves communicating your wishes to your loved ones. This involves having open, honest conversations about your wishes for your possessions, your digital footprint, and your financial affairs. It's about ensuring that your loved ones are not left with uncertainty or disputes, and that your wishes are respected.

Leaving behind a clutter-free legacy is a profound act of love and consideration. It's about decluttering, planning for your possessions, managing your digital footprint, organizing your financial affairs, and communicating your wishes. As we continue our journey of Swedish Death Cleaning, let's remember to consider not just the physical clutter in our lives, but also the legacy we leave behind. Let's strive to leave behind a clutter-free legacy that reflects our values, respects our loved ones' time and emotional well-being, and honors the life we've lived.

4. Passing Down Memories, Not Clutter

One of the most beautiful aspects of Swedish Death Cleaning is the focus on passing down memories, not clutter. It's about understanding that our most precious legacy is not our possessions, but the memories, values, and lessons we leave behind.

When we think about the items we want to pass on to our loved ones, it's often the items with sentimental value that come to mind. These are the items that tell a story, that hold a memory, that represent a piece of our lives. These are the items that our loved ones will cherish, not because of their monetary value, but because of the memories and emotions they evoke.

However, it's important to remember that not all items with sentimental value need to be kept. Sometimes, the memory is more valuable than the item itself. In these cases, consider finding a way to preserve the memory without keeping the physical item. This could involve taking a photo of the item, writing down the story associated with it, or even creating a digital archive of memories.

When deciding which items to pass down, consider their relevance and meaning to the recipient. An item that holds great sentimental value for you may not hold the same value for your loved ones. Have open, honest conversations with your loved ones about the items you're considering passing down. This can help ensure that the items you pass on will be cherished, not seen as a burden.

Passing down memories, not clutter, also involves creating new memories with your loved ones. Instead of accumulating more possessions, focus on creating experiences and moments that your loved ones will remember. These memories will be far more valuable and meaningful than any physical item.

Remember that your most important legacy is not your possessions, but the impact you've had on the lives of others. The love you've shared, the lessons you've taught, the kindness you've shown - these are the things that your loved ones will remember. These are the things that will truly stand the test of time.

Passing down memories, not clutter, is a key aspect of Swedish Death Cleaning and legacy planning. It's about preserving and sharing memories, having open conversations with your loved ones, creating new memories, and focusing on your true legacy. As we continue our journey of Swedish Death Cleaning, let's remember to focus on the memories and experiences that truly matter, and to pass down a legacy of love, wisdom, and kindness, rather than clutter.

5. Inspiring Future Generations

The practice of Swedish Death Cleaning is not only about creating a peaceful and clutter-free environment for ourselves, but it's also about inspiring future generations. By embracing a lifestyle of simplicity and intentionality, we can set a powerful example for our children, grandchildren, and the generations to come.

When we choose to live with less, we're showing future generations that happiness and fulfillment don't come from material possessions, but from meaningful experiences and relationships. We're teaching them to value quality over quantity, and to appreciate the beauty in simplicity.

By decluttering our homes and our lives, we're demonstrating the importance of making intentional choices. We're showing them that every item in our home should serve a purpose or bring us joy, and that it's okay to let go of the things that no longer do. We're teaching them to be mindful of their consumption, to consider the impact of their purchases, and to choose items that align with their values.

Through our legacy planning, we're showing future generations the importance of preparing for the future and considering the impact of our decisions on others. We're teaching them to communicate their wishes clearly, to manage their possessions responsibly, and to consider the emotional and practical burdens they may leave behind.

By passing down memories instead of clutter, we're teaching future generations to value experiences over possessions. We're showing them that our most precious legacy is not our material wealth, but the memories, values, and lessons we leave behind.

The practice of Swedish Death Cleaning is a powerful way to inspire future generations. By embracing a lifestyle of simplicity and intentionality, decluttering our homes and our lives, planning our legacy, and passing down memories instead of clutter, we can set a powerful example for our children, grandchildren, and the generations to come. As we continue our journey of Swedish Death Cleaning, let's remember to not only create a peaceful and clutter-free environment for ourselves, but also to inspire future generations to do the same.

Conclusion

MAINTAINING A CLUTTER-FREE LIFE

As we draw to the end of our journey through Swedish Death Cleaning, I want to leave you with some final thoughts and guidance. The journey of decluttering and simplifying your life is an ongoing one, and it's important to keep the momentum going.

Keeping the decluttering momentum involves regularly reassessing your possessions and your lifestyle. It's about being mindful of new purchases and only bringing items into your home that add value or bring joy. It's about continuing to make intentional choices, and remembering the peace and fulfillment that a clutter-free home brings.

Remember, decluttering is not a one-time event, but a lifelong practice. It's not about achieving a perfectly minimalist home overnight, but about making consistent, intentional choices that move you closer to a simpler, more intentional life. Be patient with yourself, celebrate your progress, and remember that every item you remove is one step closer to a clutter-free home and life.

Living with less and loving it is about embracing the beauty of simplicity. It's about finding joy in the everyday moments, appreciating what you have, and understanding that the most meaningful moments in life often come from the simplest things. It's about redefining success and fulfillment, and finding joy in the journey itself.

Living with less is not about deprivation, but about abundance. It's about freeing yourself from the burden of unnecessary possessions and commitments, and creating space for what truly matters. It's about living a life that reflects your values, and finding joy, peace, and fulfillment in the process.

Passing on the practice of Swedish Death Cleaning is about inspiring future generations. It's about setting a powerful example of simplicity and intentionality, and teaching future generations to value experiences over possessions. It's about leaving behind a legacy of love, wisdom, and kindness, rather than clutter.

Passing on the practice of Swedish Death Cleaning is not just about teaching future generations to declutter, but about inspiring them to live intentional, meaningful lives. It's about showing them that happiness and fulfillment come from within, not from material possessions. It's about teaching them to make intentional choices, to appreciate the beauty in simplicity, and to cherish the memories and experiences that truly matter.

The journey of Swedish Death Cleaning is a powerful one. It's about decluttering, simplifying, and living intentionally. It's about finding joy in simplicity, creating a clutter-free legacy, and inspiring future generations. As we close this book, I hope you feel empowered and inspired to continue your journey of Swedish Death Cleaning.

This journey is not just about decluttering your home, but about transforming your life. It's about letting go of the unnecessary, and embracing the beauty of less. It's about creating a home and a life that reflect your values, and finding joy, peace, and fulfillment in the process.

Thank you for joining me on this journey. I hope this book has provided you with the tools, inspiration, and guidance you need to embrace the practice of Swedish Death Cleaning and create a clutter-free home and life. Remember, the journey of Swedish Death Cleaning is not a destination, but a lifelong journey. Keep the momentum going, embrace the beauty of simplicity, and pass on the practice to future generations. Here's to living with less, and loving it.

Made in the USA
Las Vegas, NV
24 February 2025

18625797R00075